For Solomon,
whose undying love and faith
enabled me to complete this project.

HOW NOT TO EAT PORK©
(or life without the pig)

Written & Illustrated by
Shahrazad Ali

4th Printing

CIVILIZED PUBLICATIONS
2019 SOUTH 7TH ST.
PHILADELPHIA, PA 19148

HOW NOT TO EAT PORK
(or life without the pig)

Copyright © 1985 by Shahrazad Ali
First Edition

Printed in the United States of America
Library of Congress Cataloging in Publication Data

Ali, Shahrazad, 1947
   How not to eat pork, or, Life without the pig.

   Bibliography: p.
   Includes index.
   1. Pork-free diet.   2. Food additives.   3. Drugs.
4. Cosmetics.   I. Title.
TX373.A49 1985   613.2'6   85-70171
ISBN #0-933405-00-6 (pbk.)

Published by:
CIVILIZED PUBLICATIONS
2019 SOUTH 7TH ST.
PHILADELPHIA, PA 19148

NOTICE
If you are interested in using
   HOW NOT TO EAT PORK (or life without the pig)©
as a fundraiser for your group, church or organization
   please write to the publisher.
WHOLESALE RATES AVAILABLE

ACKNOWLEDGEMENTS

The author wishes to express her appreciation to the following persons who gave willingly of their patience, support and agreement. It was their generous assistance and valuable cooperation that helped make this book possible.

My family and children, Pam, Hassan, and Fatima Ali
SALI'S JEWELS, Philadelphia, PA
Mrs. Valerie Wallace, DELTA SIGMA THETA SORORITY, St. Louis, MO
Dr. Gloria Scott, Vice President of CLARK COLLEGE, Atlanta, GA
Najiyyah Ali, Fellow writer, UNIV. of CINCINNATI, Cincinnati, OH
Mr. Geary Jefferson, XEROX CORPORATION, Atlanta, GA
Karen Smith and Debra Yoshimura, TEMPORARIES, INC., Washington, DC
Al Garrison, Actor, Buffalo, New York
Ms. Marian Elbert, HARVARD UNIVERSITY, Cambridge, MA
Maurice B. Henderson, Playwright, Los Angeles, CA
John Eaton, Esquire, LAWYERS FOR THE ARTS, Atlanta, GA
Mr. James Wright, WRIGHT PUBLISHING CO., Atlanta, GA
Brenda Banks, Ruth Harris, Lillian Bittaye and Robin Grant, Friends
Olivette "Khalida" Smith and Mrs. Gertrude "Shane" Mitchell
Rowanda Isaf, ISAF and SHULMAN/Literary Agents, Atlanta, GA

We must debunk the pig . . .

The controversy among people as to what pork is, how it looks, and what it does to the human body knows no educational boundaries or class distinctions. The hog fan ranks from among the highly educated in our society to the most illiterate. Some justify their reasons for eating pork in very elite and sophisticated terms, down to just unabashed, blatant determination. Explanations run the gamut of blank ignorance to pitiful resignation. The average person in America has no idea how *not* to eat pork.

The Author

CONTENTS

Hog Juice
Fat meat
Wives cooking
Stopping your car

*How to Avoid Eating Pork in Restaurants
and Other Public Places*

Deciphering menues
Restaurant decor
The "grill"
Salad Bars
The Smell of pork in restaurants
Breakfast away from home
Buffets
Fast Food Chains
Parties/Dinners
Smorgasboards
Dieting
On the street interviews
What to watch
Desserts
Opening your mouth
Community dinners
Conversation
Children
Birthday parties
Nurseries
Public and Private Schools
Office protocol
Thought for today

*How to Survive When Visiting Friends
and Relatives who Eat Pork*

The Problems
Emotional Issues
Attitudes
Some of the solutions
Back against the wall
The Away-From-Home-morning-hog-blues
Dishwashers

NOTE: Chapter titles are used only to indicate main categories. Each section will cover a variety of topics related to the major subject.
The words *Pork* and *Hog* are used interchangeably in reference to the pig.

PREFACE

I remember once going out on a very special date with a very refined and marvelous man. We attended a premier play and ended the evening by going to dinner on a quietly floating river boat. We sat at the table swaying ever so slightly with the tide and chatting by candlelight. I was in heaven. The waiter came, took our order and almost immediately returned carrying two tiny bowls of the most delicious looking ice-cream I had ever seen. I wondered why he served the dessert first, but not wanting to appear ignorant or ill-mannered I graciously picked up my spoon, which was made of finely carved silver, plunged it right into my "ice cream" and stuck it quaintly into my waiting mouth. The instant the spoon touched my lips I immediately discovered what I had just crammed into my mouth was not "ice cream" but one giant scoop of whipped, fluffy butter! I tried to smile and wish it away, but it was too late, the damage was already done. This ranks as one of the most embarassing moments of my life.

I realized then that I had been literally "eating in the dark." Failing to examine what you are eating can land you in much worse jam than the one I experienced, (although I doubt it) and we do ourselves much bodily harm by diving into our plates without stopping to think; just what exactly is this?

I became more and more dissatisfied about consuming foods and using concoctions on my body that I didn't know the origin of. It was this dilemma that prompted me to write How Not To Eat Pork (or life without the pig). I had already heard some things about pork as a child and shied away from it because of this, but it remained a dangling unanswered question surrounded by much speculation but never settled. So I embarked on a pork-free diet hunt searching for pork in my foods, cosmetics, medications and accessories. What I found amazed me and I decided to share my study with others.

1

A lot of my readers will give up the hog immediately and accept this knowledge as all conclusive, still others will claim it's circumstantial evidence and not worth the bother. But you owe it to yourself to investigate any potential to improve your health and lengthen your life.

Listen carefully, we have found ourselves in a very unique position with each other when encountering discussions about pork with pork-eaters and non-pork-eaters. If a non-pork-eater refuses to eat pork in the presence of a pork-eater, he will usually be met with resentment. The hog-eaters will want everyone around them to join them in the eating of the swine. You must have a strong determination to reject something as popular as pork. You can't just say ab-bra-ca-dab-bra and make it disappear from your table. As with any other achievement earned through perserverance, you must first pay some dues. These particular dues will be redicule, envy and mockery, from your peers, and sometimes your family.

This book will help you make up your own mind about pork and allow you to make a more intelligent decision about using it other than "I've been eating it all my life." The language used is contemporary and plain. There is no scientific low-blow wording to confuse the issue or limit understanding.

This is the first time in American history this information and instructions has been revealed and made available to the consuming public. My information comes from books, medical findings, consumer interviews and my own personal observations. It is not presented to create havoc with the pork industry or medical science, but instead as a helpmate to those who have already chosen to give up the pig, or suspect they should but don't know how.

And lastly, this knowledge is offered to the multitudes of people who claim they don't eat pork, but who consume it daily in a variety of other forms, thereby making their claims at the most, superficial, an at the least — untrue. Because as you'll soon learn, it's virtually all around us.

So hold on to your plate (and your stomach) you are now invited to find out just what's involved in living without the pig.

And yes, there *IS* life after pork.

CHAPTER I

The Case Against PORK

3

THE PIG'S RESUME

OBJECTIVE: Definition of a pig.

NAME: Pig, hog, also listed as suines/swine, gilt, sow, boar and shoat. Family of Suidae, Mammals.

FROM: West Asia, the caves and hills of Europe.

CAN BE REACHED: On farms, in scientific laboratories and in some homes being used as pets.

AGE: On the planet for a little over 4,000 years.

WEIGHT: 100 to 500 pounds adult weight/ready for slaughter.

HEIGHT: 6" to 5' tall, up to 6' in length.

RACE/COLOR: White, black or brown outer skin, pale pink flesh, turns gray after death, covered with brown or black thorny bristles 1" to 6" long. Amount of hair varies with climate.

LANGUAGE: Oinks, squeaks, snorts, screeches and growls.

PHYSICAL CONDITION: Short legs, cloven hooves, cartilaginous snout (nose) small beady eyes, pointed floppy ears, sharp pointed teeth. pock marked acne skin.

AVAILABILITY: In supermarkets, bars, school cafeterias, hospitals, fast food chains, restaurants and private home kitchens.

HISTORY: Known to contain the Trichina (pork worm) throughout its entire body which is transferred to humans through the eating of its flesh.

EXPERIENCE: Every part of its body is either eaten or used to make medications, cosmetics, toiletries and personal household items.

4

ALLERGIES: NONE. Able to eat anything chewable, rotten garbage, human or animal refuse; can swallow lye or be bitten by a poisonous snake and will not die.

CERTIFICATIONS: Approved for human use and consumption by the United States Department of Agriculture and the Food and Drug Administration.

HANDICAPS: Has a tube like opening in its forelegs (similar to a sewer line) which oozes pus. Pus is a yellowish sticky white fluid formed in infected tissue. It consists of cellular debris which makes the pig's flesh sticky, greasy and slimy, especially after cooking.

SOCIAL IMPURITY NUMBER: There are some 87 breeds in existence.

AVOCATIONAL INTERESTS: Enjoys eating and rooting around on the ground looking for foodstuffs, loves to wallow in mud (water or own urine) eating anything within reach and not nailed down.

CRIMINAL RECORD: Previously charged with causing and contributing to high blood pressure, heart disease, stiff and sore muscles, strokes, obesity and Trichinosis (pork worm poisoning). Found guilty.

FUTURE ASPIRATIONS: Desires to be eaten and admired by every Homo-sapien on earth.

MOST RECENT ACCOMPLISH-MENT: Has managed to convince the public to ignore the existence of the parasite Trichinae worm in it flesh, disregard the debilitating symptoms humans suffer from eating it, and accept its presence as a natural part of the American diet.

5

REFERENCES: Recommended to be used as food by many doctors, dietitians, chefs, cooks, friends, relatives and lovers. Meat markets strongly suggest purchasing and spreading it among family members.

Note:

More detailed curriculum vitae can be found listed in encyclopedias, medical journals, health books, religious texts and the like.

Of course on physical analysis, the most detrimental element in the pig's flesh is the trichinae worm, sometimes called Trichinella; which is a parasite worm most commonly referred to as the "pork worm." This trichinae worm is found in various parts of the pig's body and when humans eat pork (no matter what grade) these microscopic worms are transferred to the mouth, stomach, intestines and eyes of the person who has swallowed it. These larvae mature within 5-7 days at which time they set up residence in the muscles of the human body. As their life cycle is completed, they become encysted in the internal organs of the host. When they die (if they do), they calcify and become tiny hardened chalk like nodules. The brain of the host may also be severely infected and there may be additional neurological problems.

Although you are unable to detect them with the naked eye (in most cases), pathologists have reported it is possible for almost a half-million trichinae to be found lodged in each pound of muscle tissue of a host. Many of these worms can be seen on x-ray after the larvae have formed cysts in the muscles (which can protect them for up to two years), after they become impregnated with chalk from calcification. They can be detected in the neck, shoulders, knees, feet and hands. (and lungs).

The female larvae is capable of laying up to 1500 eggs per day and by releasing them into the blood stream they burrow into the individual muscle fibers within a few weeks time and we suffer from their presence for years to come.

Pathologists also report that on autopsy when examining the muscles and organs of a pork-eater they are found still living and eating away on the corpse. In the case of the trichinae, which often invade the muscles of the heart, spinal cord and brain, they cause a multitude of ailments in the form of organ and circulatory distresses. When these worms invade the eyes of the pork-eater they turn the white parts red or a dull brown. Each mouthful of pork that is eaten contains clusters of these nematode worms.

A mild case of trichinosis is diagnosed as a patient having "low worm burdens" or being trichinized (infected with worms) causing a high level of eosinophils (a type of white blood cell) in the blood. Heart failure results from large numbers of larvae invading the arteries and muscles of the heart. In some medical journals these worms are referred to as trichinella spiralis. Under a microscope they look like tiny strands of white thread. I saw them for myself.

I have compiled a list of the most common illnesses that the daily eating of swine causes. Mind you, I have great respect for the medical profession in America, but I must warn you before reading this chart that your doctor will probably not agree with these findings. In fact, doctors will tell you that medical science cannot prove these illnesses are caused from the eating of pork — but they can't disprove it either. Their studies measure pressure and heart rate, not organ or muscle content. If they did measure muscle content as a standard test they would find that the male nematode measures 1.5 x 0.05 mm. and the female at 3.5 x 0.06 mm. in the flesh of a pork-eater.

You would be wise to stop eating this animal on your own, just in case it turns out to be one of those "medical conclusions" that has to be retracted. It'll save a lot of sickness now, and disappointment later.

A statistical expert who specializes in the contents of the American diet informed me that the average American consumes about 20-25 pounds of lard or shortening per year. This total does not include the actual eating of the pork meat itself.

It's not a very pleasant thought to think that when a hog-eater goes for a massage the masseur is rubbing and redistributing worms throughout their flesh. If you take the time to look this worm up in the encyclopedia or a medical dictionary and see what it actually looks like, and imagine hundreds, thousands, maybe even millions of these parasites floating around in your body and attaching themselves to your muscles it would help greatly in the ceasing to eat this meat.

"Low Worm Burdens"

COMMON ILLNESSES	BODY SYMPTOMS	PROBABLE CAUSE
Hypertension/Heart burn	Sudden onset of throbbing headache, dizziness, shortness of breath, severe chest pain	Eating pork fast that contains a lot of fat. Arteries clogged with trichinae.
Hot/Cold Sweats	Hot or cold flushes immediately after eating pork.	Poison pork shocks your bodily systems and it rebels and tries to throw off the poison through the pores.
Tiredness	No energy, weary all the time. Referred to as lazy.	Hog meat worm dragging you down, brief attacks of trichinosis.
Bloodshot eyes	Red or brown eyes, dark colored broken veins in the whites of the eyes.	The pork worm (trichinella) has invaded the eyeballs and are often close to the surface forcing the veins to protrude.
Obesity (overweight)	Big and fat, exceeding the recommended weight for your height and age. Pot guts, wide rear ends.	Eating too much fatty pork and this fat stays in the body and is not passed as body waste. The waste stays inside of you.
Back, neck, shoulder and headache, joint pains	Stiffness and soreness in joints, cracking bones, aching and swollen limbs, aggravation on movement.	The trichinae worms have calcified (hardened) inside your muscles and tendons making it difficult for you to move around.

8

Body odors and bad breath

Sweat smells overly offensive, breath stinks, (mouth tastes bad to self) Sour stomach.

The rank odor of the swine has been absorbed into your system and seeps out through the pores of your skin.

Uncontrollable Temper

Easy to rile, hard to calm down, heavy breathing when angry, quick to act savage, or exhibit wild and destructive behavior.

The brain has become infested with pork worms, causing the host to take on the characteristics of the hog — shameless, bullified, bold, greedy, and impatient as the nervous system is affected.

Aging, pimpled skin, offensive smelling fecal matter, excess mucus in the body cavities, and rotted teeth and gums are also promoted by the constant eating of the swine.

The medical diagnostic terms used to describe these maladies are:

Weakness and malaise
Trunk and limb edema
Subconjuctival hemorrhages
Dysphagia/hoarseness
Subinguinal splinter hemorrhages
Myalgia
Fulminant enteritis
Cysticercosis (tapeworm)
Brucellosis

Subcutaneous rashes (macular)
Periorbital edema
Myositis
Prostration
Fever of Unknown Origin
Emesis and Cephalgia
Hypertension
Pork Tapeworm (Taenia)
Diarrhea

Evaluate your own medical history and see how many of the following symptoms you are currently suffering from! Many have experienced these symptoms which possibly have been misdiagnosed by a physician or deemed as untreatable.

Just because the trichinae worm is microscopic do not assume that they are harmless. In large enough quantities they do much harm, and certainly when they breed in clusters they cause the body much distress.

Public Health Survey reports say only about 300,000 people are actually infected with trichinosis each year is only partly true. Only about 300,000 are actually reported, there are millions who suffer from the "low worm burdens" of headache, upset stomach, muscle aches, red eyes, and diarrhea who never report these symptoms to their doctor because they believe them to be caused by other reasons.

Another area of concern is prenatal diet. The idea that a woman with child can eat just about anything she craves for has proven to be deceptively insignificant. If you are pregnant and eating pork you can be sure you are transmitting the trichinae parasite (pork worm) to your unborn baby since your baby in its fetal state derives all of its nourishment from your body and its flesh is made from your flesh. If you are nursing you expose your baby to the same risk by transferring these microscopic worms to your baby through your milk. The trichinae worm easily travels through your circulatory system and attaches itself to anything fleshy it can cling to — including the baby in your stomach. Who know what kind of problems and/or long range difficulties this causes a newborn. Perhaps soon someone will investigate this. In the meantime, stop eating pork on your own, before and after you have your child.

Despite what health officials or farmers say, cooking does not kill these nasty worms, and even if heat did destroy them, the thought of eating cooked filthy parasites is not appealing.

Although the USDA and FDA have seemingly admirable intentions by going around with their little blue stamp pads, it is totally impossible for these agents to properly check the millions upon millions of pigs currently being approved to be sold and eaten. No way. There ar too many breeders, breeds, and slaughter houses located on thousands of farms in thousands of locations.

It seems as if the money in "pigging" is so big that very few authority figures will take a stand and call a pig a pig. So whether or not they tell us to cook it at 185°F of at the new temperature of 170°F is of no consequence when depending on heat to kill these worms.

Some of this pork (most of it) is labeled as "cured" and in order for something to require being "cured" it has to have some kind of disease or ailment to begin with. Curing pork is traced back to the ancient Greek. They used acorns, peaches and peanuts which when mixed together created a concoction which allegedly "cured" pig meat of the filth in its flesh. Of course, it didn't work for them either and many of their people suffered fatal cases of trichinosis.

Dietitians will often remark "it's okay to eat a little pork as long as you cook it done and eat only the lean portions" but in actuality it is usually only the hypertensive patients who receive any instructions at all about eating pork. Everyone should be instructed and warned, and told to stop eating it irregardless of their present health status.

I know of families who have certain members who suffer from high blood pressure and they told me they often have to literally hide the pork. Some of these hypertensives sneak and eat some whenever they get a chance, knowing full well they will have to suffer the physical consequences afterward. This is sad, but many, especially our oldsters have developed a taste for pork stemming back to their childhoods when their meals were filled with cracklin' bread (a cornbread with bits of chopped up pork cooked in it), fried bacon rind and souse meat. It is extremely difficult to convert and change these people's minds about eating pork.

We must continue to work on these old folks and even though we don't have as much control over their diets (which is sometimes based on their finances), as we would like; we definitely have control over our own diets, and the upcoming generation's. They are counting on us to give them clear directives on food choices and proper nutrition, in order to preserve their lives and assure that each oncoming generation will live longer than the one preceding it.

I was pleased to learn during my patient interviews with hypertensive men and women that many had given up eating pork on their own accord. They commented they found the giving up of salt more difficult than the pork meat itself, but gave ready testimony about what happened to them whenever they did slip and eat some. The worse complaint was the pounding, maddening headache and the dizziness often bordering on vertigo. They also said they believed their symptoms stymied from more than just eating sodium or salt because they never had the same reaction from eating potatoe chips, popcorn snacks, or fried chicken from a carry-out. All of these three foods contain a very high level of salt and sodium.

Often times I would attempt to question their physicians about eating pork and the harmful affects of the worm it contained. Many report they find it preferable not to treat what they diagnose as "low worm burdens" in patients who have accompanying symptoms of something else more treatable and whose "low worm burdens" are not particularly permanently debilitating. I hope you'll agree that the symptoms I described on the previous chart have been mighty debilitating to us all.

I found that many of the younger physicians, especially residents, were more apt to agree that their patients should stop eating pork altogether. Many of them agreed that the information in this book is an excellent contemporary deterrent from eating pork and promised to recommend it to their patients, families and friends. We shall see.

So that you will know which meats are "pork" I have included a sample list of how it's offered to us in the supermarkets:

Sausage	Hog maws
Bacon	Pig tails
Ham	Pork brains
Chopped Ham	Pig ears
Meat Bologna	Pig feet
Pepperoni	Fat back
Salami	Ham hocks (pig knuckles)
Streak-o-lean	Pork tripe
Meat franks/weiners	Pork liver
Corn dogs	Pork kidneys
Pork chops	Hog heads
Pork ribs	Hog snouts (noses)
Pork steaks	Hog head cheese
Pork loin	Chitterlings/chittlins

Neck bones	Swine testicles (Mountain
Pig Tongues	Oysters)
Pork tenderloin	Pork cutlets

These are the most popular cuts. In some places they still sell the pig's lungs, thyroid and esophagus. Some of the above parts are left out in the open, salted down and allowed to harden to be used as seasonings. To keep up with modern times and new styled meat processing, we have now been presented with "sow nuggets" and to top it all off there's a new frozen chittlin' T.V. dinner in your freezer case.

You can rarely go shopping and not see at least one of these pieces of the pig's cadaver in someone's cart. Nowadays we have been told that if we remove the fat from the pork and take away the salt that it is just as nutritious and wholesome as any other meat. Don't believe it.

Pork is supposed to be rich in B-vitamins, thiamine, riboflavin and rich in iron. But it's also rich in some nasty little critters called trichinae.

Man's search for food has led to the experimental eating of all sorts of things formerly defined as garbage. Some pig proponents proudly proclaim jokingly they eat "the hair off the hog." They do too. Because a great deal of the tails, feet and especially the ears still have some of the black bristles of the pig's hair on the surface. I asked several people in big city supermarkets what they did about the hair on the pig's ear and they told me not to worry, they fall right out after the meat is done!

These ears, feet, noses, stomachs and limbs also have a lot of scars and sores on them and other rotten looking marks. I was told that these were also cooked "as is" and not cut off before eating or being ground into sausage. Yuck.

These pigs can have:

cholerea	Nasal Catarrh
strangles	mange
quinsy	measles
colic	brucellosis
diarrhea	swine pox
splenitis	diseased livers
thumps	peritonitis
lice	and blind staggers

13

These maladies sound ominous enough to bring a lump in your throat. The consumer is never advised of these possibilities. Understandably. Nobody, I repeat, NOBODY, can guarantee you 100% that the pork you purchase has not been exposed to or contaminated by at least two of the aforementioned maladies. Butchers handle infected pork freely and do not wash their hands after touching it and move right on to the next unaware customer who may be purchasing beef — which may have several microscopic trichinae worms attached to it.

Now it appears to me that since we cannot rely on our health officials to warn us against eating pork that we must take this task on for ourselves and begin constructing a diet that is swine-free. We can police it ourself, control it ourself and endorse it ourself. The major requirement for doing this is to *pay attention*. Pay attention to what our food tastes like, smells like and how it was prepared.

Dealing with the slam-bam issues of day to day survival can leave little time to concern oneself with what to eat, when to eat and where it came from, but the paying attention system will eliminate flagrant and random eating habits immediately.

There has been no progress made in discovering a way to produce a trichina-free pork in the past 150 years of modern research. Knowledge of the trichina worm's existence, and the harm it causes the human body, is one of the least publicized medical problems in this country. The major symptoms are so flu-like that this problem has been absorbed into other categories. There is a great deal of money involved in the pork trade in its entirety, and unfortunately, public apathy has prevented a thorough examination or presentation of information regarding this particular nematode.

I have seen and studied these horrible little monsters in a scientific laboratory, and very well understand how they are able to be disregarded and go undetected for so long, because the porkworm deteriorates the body from the inside out — steadily. It is a very slow moving but aggressive parasite that multiplies rapidly even envading the human tongue, diaphragm, and sometimes found in the secretions emitted from sores on the body of a pork-eater. They have equally been reported to be living deep within the eardrum. I will never forget the sight of them for as long as I live. Seeing this worm in fresh pork, pork purchased from a standard grocery, and in the brain and selected muscles of the deceased, convinced me to complete this project.

This first chapter is a bit harsher than the following ones but in order for you to understand exactly what we're dealing with and what's at stake, I was forced to give you a double dose of anti-pork medicine all in one gulp. Now we can get on to the crux of this issue which is HOW *NOT* TO EAT PORK and live a life without the pig. Read this chapter twice if you must because as you proceed through the balance of this text you may possibly need to recall some of these facts.

CHAPTER II

How did humans start eating the pig?

For several thousand years the pig was eaten and used almost exclusively by the caveman in Europe, this was thousands of more years before they migrated to other parts of the planet. When the white man came to America, he brought some pigs with him.

When Black people were enticed and forced to come to American in or around the year of 1500, the slavemasters raised hogs on the plantation along with other livestock. The slavemaster and his family ate the chops, the roasts, the loins and the hams. They threw out the undesirable innards of the pig such as the intestines, the bowel sack, the liver, the brain, the head, tail, hooves and ears. Blacks caught and ate this fatty offal because it was all that was available to them. It certainly broke the monotony of a starchy and non-protein diet that made up the slaves' customary menu. The slavemaster ate "high" on the hog and the poor slave ate "low" on the hog. Whites have continued to eat this animal which was shipped to America with their forefathers. Once Blacks reached the status of being physically free, they also continued to eat the "low" on the hog and many can now afford to eat "high" on the hog, but it's still hog, still filth and still a habit cultivated in a people during the most horrible period of existence this race has ever experienced. But instead of associating hog eating with the bad times, they now use it to celebrate the good times like Christmas, New Year's, Easter and at parties.

The reasons given for continuing to use pork for food usually contain something like "pigs are now fed better and they don't just eat filth anymore." Well, let me shed a little light on that comment; neither farmers or scientists have discovered a way to manufacture or breed a pig that does not contain the trichinae worm. No! It has not and cannot be done. If they feed them caviar and champagne they still would not be fit to eat.

Cows and sheep are a different breed, they are mild, non-aggressive and vegetarians. Pigs are vegetarian, carnivorous and cannibalistic. They eat whatever they can get their mouths on, including their own babies.

In America and other countries, it used to be unlawful to slaughter and immediately eat a pig. (Sometimes referred to as a green-hog.) Of course, like many of our other food certification laws, this one was not strictly adhered to or monitored for compliance. Our Federal agencies know that a pig is totally unfit to eat right after it has been killed and they have to have considerable processing before being considered edible. Not even the rabbit is forced to submit to such strenuous regulations, and rabbits are from the rodent (like in rat) family. But it is much better to eat a rabbit, a cat or a dog, than to eat a hog.

The hog is a scavenger much like the buzzard — and when is the last time you heard of anyone eating a buzzard? A snail maybe. A rattlesnake, an octopus or an insect, but never a buzzard. At least we all just about agree on that.

Remember, a person who eats an animal who eats anything it can find — will eat anything, period. Every item on the planet that can be chewed should not necessarily be used for food.

Recently the pork industry has been advertising and telling the public to dispel and not believe the "rumors" circulating regarding the problems caused from eating pork. 1983 was supposed to be the year of the hog. I'm glad it wasn't. They are advertising to strengthen their acceptance and promote sales. The Federal Trade Commission (FTC) does not allow the cigarette industry to advertise on the airways anymore, because they and the Surgeon General have determined that tobacco is harmful to our health. The pig should be added to this list because it too is harmful to our health. The cigarette industry turned to other visual aides such as billboards, field promotions, special sales people and magazine advertisements. We all know that a good advertising campaign is a formidable opponent in a country where point of eye contact is of first importance. Our most popular products are always pleasing to the eye. Generic brands in the grocery stores are usually a last-choice selection. They have been called sterile, unattractive and boring, as if when purchasing a foodstuff we plan to eat the package too. What is pleasing to the eye is not always pleasing to the body.

I do give the pork industry credit for one important thing. They, themselves, warn hog-eaters about the imminent dangers of eating/handling pork. They use to caution their customers to wash their hands thoroughly after handling raw pork, and to also wash any dishes or counter tops it has come into contact with while in the raw stage. There in *no other* common American food on the market that requires the eater to take these types of precautions — before eating it! Although the Surgeon General has not pointed the finger at pork, just like tobacco, the consumer is advised to partake at your own risk. The decision to eat pork is not on the suppliers, it is on the consumers.

Eventually, in years to come, we can expect to see such Federal warning labels on salt and sugar too. Many are already well on their way to eliminating these two seasoners from their diets.

There are so many new diets on the market making it more confusing for the consumer to make a decision. One says eat meat, another says eat vegetables, some others say eat neither and a few even suggest eating so much fiber it's likened to swallowing sandpaper confetti.

Any food eaten in controlled and reasonable portions can function as diet food. That is, any food except pork.

These pigs that many are currently eating have been made both cute and attractive by cartoonists and artists in children's books where they depict the pig as pretty pink and cherub like, mild mannered and friendly. These descriptions are not at all what a pig really looks like and acts like. It's unfortunate that our small children are introduced to the nature of the pig in this way while they are young and impressionable.

The pig is classified as a grafted animal. Grafted means when you take traits from one thing, mix it with the traits of another, and the final product from this mixture is something completely different from what you started out with. i.e., a grapefruit is grafted from an orange and a lemon; a mule is grafted from a female donkey and a male horse. Well the pig is grafted from the cat, rat and the dog. The final product (a pig) does indeed have the worse traits of all of these animals, one shrewd, one greedy, and one sneaky — and all germ infested. It's also listed that it evolved from the hippopotamus and rhinocerous.

This pig has been roaming the earth for about 4,000 years. Moses used this newly designed garbage disposal to clean up the filth surrounding the hills and caves of Europe. At that time the hog's major purpose, other than eating filth, was for medicinal purposes. Hog is said to be a handy aid in curing boils, burns, and the erythematous swelling following a black-eye (some use steak for this — which is better). Pork has also been used to bond amputated fingers or toes back on to the limb they were severed from, and as a bandage on burn victims, it peels off easily.

Even the cave people did not start out using the hog for food, although they roamed freely and were quite plentiful.

Today, people all over the world have developed taste buds that are so perverted they desire to experience this taste of the hog practically all day and all night. Some have inducted it so firmly into their lifestyles they eat it so routinely as to ignore its' presence. This pork issue has remained a stumbling block, and quite a serious one at that because eating it has interfered with the unification of certain groups. Some want to eat it and claim it's fun, while others want no part of it — under any circumstances.

Anyway, even though the european brought the pig with him (the Eurasian Pig) when he came to America, it was not an easy task, (note: I found so many explanations as to where the American pig came from that I decided its place of origin is not as important as the reality that they are here in our midst and need to be reckoned with), the settlers had a hard time controlling them because the pigs made attempts and often succeeded at maiming and killing off the other live-stock. Eventually, they re-bred them and created a more controllable and domestic hog that would not be such a bully. The Indians were not eating pigs when the first white settlers arrived here — they didn't even know what one was. They were into buffalo, bear, snakes and fish. Pretty soon they and the rest of the people soon not only knew what a pig was but began to accept its odd taste and utilize its various parts for food.

The pig still functioned as the garbage disposal during early American times, they ate what was generally called "slop" which contained scraps of food, trash, human and animal refuse, rotten vegetables and the like. They got rid of it quickly, saved the farmer money by not requiring special feed, and remained in one spot waiting for the next bucket of "slop" to be dumped in their sty. They never required the presence of a "pigherder" to keep up with them.

It seems that pigs have been here just as long as we have, so the redirecting of our taste buds and restyling of our daily menus calls for a major overhaul in our eating habits. We must begin in each home, at every table, to make plans and decisions to stop this pig-symptom genocide from overpowering us. We must not continue to jeopardize the lives, health and well-being of nearly 300 million Americans just for the sake of eating pork.

I will not dignify the response of "I've been eating it all my life, and so has my mother and my grandmother, and they lived to be 195 years old," with any attempts to debate this absurd attitude and preposterous outdated assumption that habit equals correctness. When we learn better we must do better. This is incumbent upon each individual who desires to live a healthier and cleaner life.

The profiteering connected to pork is so successful that it's deemed economically couterproductive to ends its use. Any large conglomerate, no doubt, has a very difficult time when it comes to arriving at a choice between telling the truth and making some money. Especially if the people have become apathetic about the product and continue to use it because of lack of national attention to the harm it causes.

This is not an attack on the thousands of employees who work in the pork industry trying to earn a living, but they too should be made aware of the inherent danger of eating and handling pork.

CHAPTER III

What Do Religious Scholars Say About the Pig?

To put it bluntly, the Bible directly forbids the eating or touching of the pig. The christian religion teaches that Jesus cast the devil (evil and filth) into the hog. This passage clearly states Jesus' position on the pig. Many religious scholars/ clergy quickly dismiss this warning by saying: "that was before we had proper refrigeration to preserve pork so it would not spoil" but that's not exactly what it says in the Bible, and this accuses Jesus of being ignorant of the future and spreading temporary teachings.

The parts in the Bible that give clear instructions to reject the pig are the only parts of the Bible that Bible followers in America reserve the right to reinterpret. Most believers take the truth of the Bible to be all truth and nothing but the truth. But the eating of swine flesh is against the christian religion according to its' own teachings, yet christians are the major hog eaters on earth.

The biblical passages that give guidance on this point are verified in the following scriptures:

Rom. 12:1	Deut. 14:8
John 2	Genesis 1:29, 9:3-5
Genesis 7:2, 3,1:29	Leviticus 11:7-8
Psalms 111:8, 84:11, 119:105	Ezekiel 33:11, 22:26
Corinthians 6:20, 3:17, 10:31, 6:17	Luke 4:2,3
Isaiah 66:15-17, 2-4, 55:2	Revelations 22:11,12
Mark 5:11-16	

In the Torah passages about the pig are located in:
(Same as the Old Testament of the Christian Bible)

In the Quran it is listed under:

2:168, 173
5:3
6:122, 146, 147
16:115

I have not copied all of these passages. If you are a believer in any of the religions which adhere to these holy books, then looking up this documentation will strengthen your desire to give up the hog. Look them up for yourself and see what the holy men and prophets have to say about eating pork.

For those who are not familiar with any of these texts, it's best you consult the Holy Bible (at the library or drawer in the room of all Hotels/Motels). The Torah is available at any Synagogue, and the Quran in all Islamic Mosques.

Take note that in the entire time that organized and unorganized religion has existed, there has never been a civilized religion that advocates the eating of the swine. Neither the Bible, Torah or Quran preaches this type of doctrine, in fact, they all teach against eating hogs. The position on pork is assumed by some to be the only subject these three religious books agree on. I'm glad.

Of course for those who do not believe in any type of a God, be aware that the teachings in these three (3) Holy books were written by men — not God, who were the writers, prophets and scientists of those days who wrote documents to apply to all times and outlast the civilizations they lived in. When they received and perceived this wisdom they put it on paper. I can't imagine having a God who would send his words and instruction to provide us with knowledge, wisdom and understanding and then leave out warnings about the pig. But that didn't happen, they did warn and instruct us and many of us have disregarded these warnings because of inconvenience. It is too inconvenient for some people to give up the hog. If we follow God's directions coupled with what we have learned and experienced we would forsake this nasty creature.

Why should we eat filth and worms in the diseased flesh of the pig when there are so many other good things the Supreme Being intended for us to eat and enjoy?

Does anyone really want to go through life labeled as a hog-eater or swine supporter? These titles are not honorable sounding because the pig is not an honorable animal. His name is only used to speak of filth or nastiness: i.e., filthy as a pig, nasty as a pigpen, fat as a hog, pig-headed, hog-wild, greedy as a hog, hogging the moment, pig latin (mixed up language). All of these are the uncomplimentary slogans coined about the hog and used by those who are familiar with the savage traits and attributes of the pig.

If our houses of worship were forced to strictly adhere to their holy books it would be impossible for them to hold such affairs as Church Barbeques, Christmas Chittlin dinners, or roast pig suppers, on or near a religious house of worship. Yet most of these items are prepared in every American church kitchen, in the very pulpits of God's house. Sometimes sold and used to raise money in the name of the Lord.

Farmers have been know to hold Pig Slaughter Festivals during the hog killing seasons. Family reunion activities often are centered around roasting a pig or smoking pork ribs over a barbeque pit. At one time it was required that if you roasted a pig it was best to do so underground in a pit. As a national symbol of the pig's unquenchable appetite and his unrelinquishing greed, they are placed on a platter with an apple stuck in their mouth — even the cooks know the main trait of the pig — GREED.

Taking communion in church and eating crackers or bread that contains lard (a pork derivative) is outragious as a means of worshiping God by doing exactly what he has forbade us to do while at the same time praying for his blessings. Yet eating pork in church is as natural as passing the collection plate.

This appeal is to the old believers and the new believers of any religions who use the Bible, Torah or Quran as the basis of their religious teachings.

Clergymen/women are as a rule hesitant to advise their congregations against the eating of pork. Several of them told me that they do not want to sound like they are affiliated with other religions who also require that their followers do not eat pork. I found this to be an odd position to take and use as an excuse for dispensing pork to the flock, especially since it has already been proven that *ALL* religions forbid the eating of the swine (except the Hindu). A lot of the clergy I interviewed had earned Doctorates of Divinity (a D.D. degree).

While visiting a theological seminary I questioned several of the instructors about what they teach, their curriculums, schedules and priorities. As you probably guessed, eating of the swine was no where to be found as a subject for discussion or class study. I was told "it doesn't matter what you eat as long as you believe." A lot of the instructors found the entire issue humorous and only laughed at my questions. They were not as concerned with saving the body as they were with saving the soul.

I would give just about anything to hear an old fire and brimstone teaching on why we shouldn't eat pork supported by religious text.

I should add, that in the South I found several small christian sects who did no eat pork (pork meat) and these groups were pleased to find out that I didn't eat it either and invited me to stay a while to fraternize and break bread. While in the North, occasionally I would stop and talk to a few member of randomly selected congregations and once again the subject of eating pork was met with amusement. I didn't question the older adults (for reasons already mentioned), and I got the sneaking feeling that many of the interviewees between the ages of 30-50 felt they were being very liberated and modernistic in their responses when stating they "didn't care what was in it (pork) they intended to keep on eating it." It seemed they believed themselves to be exerting their own individuality and assertiveness of choice. Ever so often one or two of the quieter ones would pull me aside afterwards and say: "you know, I really don't eat it as much as I used to" or "I have a friend who says he/she gave it up and they feel much better."

Sometimes when I talked to several (up to 7-8) church members at one time I could hardly get a word in edgewise, because they would all start testifying at once about how much they loved pork, and the kinds they were particularly fond of. If I pressed further they would become uncomfortable with the subject and try to quickly change it. Some members would become embarassed and just move away from the group, and a few others refused to make direct eye contact with me while they were ranting about how much they loved the hog.

One young man, a deacon, told me he intended to keep eating pork until they tell him to stop. He never identified who "they" were, and I never asked. I tried to get into a few church kitchens but was stopped at the door, (and get this) one good sister told me that she knew of a few members who didn't eat pork when they first came to the church, but "after they hung around here for a while they started to, and now they can't get enough of it." I left.

Pork Linked to Cirrhosis

Researchers at the University of Ottawa have linked pork consumption with cirrhosis, a chronic degeneration of the liver.

In a study of 16 nations with readily available statistics for consumption of pork, beef, fat and alcohol, Dr. Amin Nanji and Dr. Samuel French found a correlation between eating pork and the incidence of cirrhosis of the liver—an even higher incidence when both pork and alcohol were consumed.

No connection was found between cirrhosis and beef consumption.

According to Dr. Nanji, writing in *The Lancet*: "The mortality rate from cirrhosis ... was directly related to per-capita pork consumption in these countries [Sweden, Norway and Finland]. In Canada the mortality from cirrhosis in each province also correlated with pork consumption but not with alcohol intake."

The researchers said that the way in which pork consumption "might cause or enhance" cirrhosis remains a mystery. Yet the team concludes that cirrhosis mortality directly relates to the amount of pork consumed.

Perhaps the researchers would do well to examine Leviticus 11:7-8: "And the swine ... , you shall not eat, and their carcasses you shall not touch. They are unclean to you" (*Revised Authorized Version*).

This warning is understood by many Jews and Muslims. So why not write for our free article "Is All Animal Flesh Good for Food?" ■ *The* PLAIN TRUTH

NEW PACK CHITLINS

Boston Butt Pork Roast

PIG FEET

Pork'N Beans

A possum in every pot

Hog

PIG EARS

SCRAPPLE?

FLESH whole

PIGS

Frozen Pork Ribs

lean ham

BY THE SLAB

PORK

FEET, TAILS OR

ALL AMERICAN WHOLE

Boneless Ham

PINKY PIG LEAN CORN FED WHOLE

eat fatback for midday meal

Oven Kahlua Pork

baby possum:

HICKORY SMOKED

High on the Hog

Canned Ham

PORK

CHAPTER IV

WHAT ELSE IS THERE TO EAT?

Of course NO animal flesh is fit for human consumption, but if you must be carnivorous eat some of the following:

Beef wieners	Filet Mignon
Beef coldcuts	Beef Bacon
Beef Ribtips	T-bone steaks
Flank Steak	Beef liver
London Broil	Beef/Ox tails
Chuck/Round Steak	Beef tenderloin
Beef Sausage	Sirloin steak
Beef roast	Chicken
Ground beef (burgers)	Lamb
Beef neckbones	Veal
Corned beef	Turkey

Fish

Compare this list with the Pork list and choose from this one to replace the pork. As civilized people, we must consider ourselves too dignified to eat the head, ears, lips, intestines, bowel sacks and feet of an animal. We have surely elevated all kinds of waste substances to the highly stature of dietary desire. If you must eat meat then eat the above kinds. They are all cleaner than the pig.

There are many beautiful vegetables which can be eaten along with your new meat choices. The list is much too numerous to outline here so I will tell you the vegetables that you should NOT eat. Any vegetables not listed are tolerable in controlled quantities.

DO NOT EAT: Collard greens
Butter beans
Lima beans
Black-eyed peas
Great Northern beans
Field Peas

These are the main "greens and beans" that you should stay away from if you have any concern at all for your stomach and lower intestines. The eating of these "vegetables" was also started during early American times. Originally they were all used for livestock feed but poverty was so abundant during that time for certain classes of people and these vegetables were transferred from the trough for the animals to the table for the humans.

These "greens and beans" are responsible for many a stomach ache and severe case of indigestion. Some have been rushed to the hospital and put on medical alert because of the symptoms caused from eating these "greens and beans." Gas (air pockets) in the stomach and intestines generated in the body from the eating of these "vegetables" can cause anything from a bloated abdomen creating the passing of foul smelling odors from the rectum, to equally foul smelling odors from the mouth in belching. The body can't contain the tremors that these "beans and greens" force it to accept. These "vegetables" were not designed to be used as human food, but are for the growth of animals, (livestock.)

Eating a plate of one of these "beans and greens" is like committing slow suicide by destroying and wearing out your internal digestive system because of the gassy side affects which accompany the eating of these items.

A lot of people who refuse to stop eating pork do so because they don't recognize the symptoms or believe they have physical proof in their own bodies. But a person could eat a pinch of cyanide every day for a year and never die from it, but eventually they would begin to feel the side affects of the poison in headaches, limb aches and upset stomachs. If they would swallow one teaspoon full of this same poison all at one time they would fall over dead on the spot. Slow death is not a better death. Dead is dead, it doesn't matter if you take the elevator or the escalator — you'll still arrive.

Another list you might be interested in is a list of some other meats which are not wholesome, but not as filthy as the hog. They are:

Possums	Squirrel
Coons	Turtles
Ducks	Frogs
Deer	Moose
Rabbits	Bear

Now look at this list. Visualize exactly what these animals look like, visualize their eating habits and their behavior and hopefully you'll come to a like conclusion that we should not eat these animals. They are just animals — not food.

You will never find a non-hog-eater cooking, cleaning or eating any of the above species, but nearly every hog-eater will eat, has already eaten, or is still eating one or more on the above list. This proves that if a person will eat a hog they most assuredly will devour anything else.

Look around, check out your colleagues and find out if they have ever eaten any of the creatures on this list. Some hunters traditionally want to eat what they have destroyed. This is not necessary to assure the animals death nor to experience the kill.

We have all heard the old saying "you are what you eat." After learning the nature of the pig and other near-nasty animals, it is no wonder many human beings are running around behaving savagely, greedy, shameless, and wallowing in filth of all kinds. Many have become so obsessed with the pig they can't help but to exemplify its traits.

I visited a pig farm during my travels to see for myself exactly how the pig now lives in captivity. They were all over the place, squirming and squeaking, snorting and slurping, nudging each other out of the way to get at a better spot around the food. Their voluminous stomachs swaying with each motion. Ugly chunky heads burrowing around on the ground, sputum running loosley down their chins, surrounded by clogs of nose mucous. They just lick it off and continue on with their business of eating and packing. Their eyes were roving around in their heads, excited at the prospect of getting something to eat. I left there understanding the full meaning of gluttony. Their impudicity was horrible.

I am so happy that we have a choice in making a decision about one of the most controversial food issues of this millenium. Some of us have a sort of confusion going on about what position we are in as a consumer. If it's in front of us, then we think we should buy it and try it. We don't have to. We can reject eating the pig in the same way we reject eating the oven cleaner or the Drano.

If you stop eating this animal for just 30 days — 1 month, you will recognize the difference in your life instantly. What is a one month sacrifice if the knowledge gained during that time will add years to your life? Take the *one* month test and see. No pork for thirty days straight. You should take this test just to see if it's possible or not. This one month test will also give you a first hand glimpse of just how much pork you come in contact with daily. This is the *30-Day-No-Hog* test. If you can, get a friend to take this test with you then you can help to support each other (and defend each other) while monitoring each other's progress.

PRODUCT NOTES

PORK
IRRADIATION

Food Safety and Inspection Service confirms final rule of 1/15/86 permitting use of gamma radiation to control trichinella spiralis in pork carcasses. Absorbed dose permitted is between .3 kiloGray and 1 kiloGray. FSIS also has published its response to comments received. Eff: 1/15/86. Inf: Ms. Margaret O'K. Glavin, 202/447-6042.

USDA announces intent to permit producers of dry cured or country ham not currently using one of the two prescribed methods for destroying trichina in pork to continue to use nonconforming methods beyond 8/6/85. Research will be conducted between now and 12/31/86 to find one or more additional effective processing methods. Eff: 6/18. Inf: B. Dennis, 202/447-3840. (FR 6/18: 25202).

FDA OKs radiation to treat pork

WASHINGTON (AP)— The Food and Drug Administration yesterday approved the use of radiation on fresh meat for the first time.

In a notice published in the Federal Register, the FDA said it would approve limited use of radiation treatments to kill Trichinella spiralis, a trichinosis-causing parasitic worm found in uncooked pork.

The FDA said last year it would consider allowing radiation to be used to control other parasites as well. However, it limited approval to use for Trichinella spiralis after the Agriculture Department questioned whether the procedure was effective in killing other contaminating parasites. SunTimes 7/23/8

Worm Section →

89¢

HAM + BEANS

Ingredients:
pig toes, Pig eyeballs,
pig testes, Pig rectums,
Ham hock, Ears + Noses.
+ Beans

HOW TO SHOP $

CHAPTER V

HOW TO SHOP WITHOUT PURCHASING ITEMS CONTAINING PORK

Obviously you can't avoid something unless you know where it is or at least be aware of where it might be lurking. A good way for you to start your transition of developing a pork-free diet is to go shopping at a time when the store is relatively empty and quiet of extra activity. This will allow you the time and privacy to read the ingredients on labels. Initially it'll take a few minutes longer than usual to shop but as you become more familiar with swine terminology things will speed up. Pretty soon you'll know which brands contain pork and which ones do not. You'll discover certain aisles you will eliminate from shopping in completely.

I wanted to give you the exact brand names of these items but I'm not trying to pick a fight with the various companies who produce these products. I have chosen to give you the product categories and leave out the brand names, but this information is sufficient for you to decipher the labels and bring home a car full of pork-free foods, cosmetics, medications and accessories. I performed my study by investigating the major brands and a few of the not too popular ones. It was frightening. Don't be paranoid, but for us to assume that everything packaged, labeled and stocked in a supermarket is "okay" for eating is a wrong assumption. We can't put that much trust in companies and people whom we don't know. These products come from places, farms and factories that we are not remotely familiar with in most cases. Yet we have grown to accept these products with the greatest of ease.

Eating pork in our foods is a cultivated habit which starts at a very early age in this country — at the infant level. Pork is contained in about half of all the baby food selections on the grocery shelves. It is programmed into us to start developing a taste for swine as early as our first introduction to solid food. By the time we are adults, we discover that the body can have needs which demand the brain to devise schemes to fulfill.

Habits picked up very early in life are extremely difficult to curtail and require a mental alarm to go off in the mind instructing the body to obey the brain and not the instinct. Such it is with the stopping of pork eating. You'll have to pay attention, and every time you open your mouth you'll have to think.

By this time everyone taking this course on "How Not To Eat Pork" should be able to recognize hog/pig selections which are out in the open, but the *hidden* hog ingredients take a bit more scrutiny.

All food products are required by law to give a list of their ingredients on the label in descending order. In other words, what the product contains the most of will be at the beginning, and what it contains the least of will be at the end. There's a lot of controversial substances between these two points. The least number of ingredients on a food label are the best ones to buy.

*The most recognizable and easiest to pronounce terms which mean pork are:

> Lard
> Animal shortening
> Gelatin
> Shortening
> Animal fats
> Hydrolyzed animal protein/protein
> Collagen or Enzymes
> Tallow

*The more difficult ones are:

> Emulsifiers
> Stabilizers (Mono and Di-glycerides)
> Tween
> Swine pepsin
> Calcium stearate
> Magnesium stearate
> Poly-sorbates
> Monostearates
> Fatty acids

---

*Write these words on the back of a business card and carry them with you at all times until you memorize them. This way you will always have a handy reference on hand to make verifications.

These are the words used to disguise and dress up a product to keep from saying "pork" or "pig" or "swine." Just looking at a product is not sufficient to determine if it contains pork because modern preservatives and colorations make it impossible to tell by looking alone what you are actually buying.

CATEGORIES OF FOODS WHICH CONTAIN PORK

FREEZER
Pot pies (oven type)
Cookie dough
Pie crust
Whipped toppings
Pastry rolls
T.V. Dinners
Pizza
Breaded products

Ice Cream
Frozen Pastries

CAN GOODS
Meats (packed in gelatin)
Baked beans
Pre-mixed frostings
Refried beans
Canned ham
Pork and beans
Ham spreads
Blackeye peas

Great Northerns
Lima Beans
Leafy greens

BOXED PRODUCTS
Soda crackers
Cake mix
Muffin mix
Graham crackers
Pastry/baking mix
Cold cereals
Cookies
Round & square
  crackers
Hot chocolate mix
Gelatin desserts
Buttered Popcorn Salt

DAIRY
Cheeses
Yogurt
Cottage cheese
Margerine
Chip dips
Frozen biscuits
Breakfast rolls
Orange cheese
Cheese spreads

PASTRY DEPT.
White bread
Wheat bread
Rye bread
Dinner rolls
Cookies
Cakes
Pies
Doughnuts

SHELF ITEMS
Jellies/jams
Gelatin desserts
Candy
Marshmallows
Fried pork rinds
Pickled pig feet
Tube cake icing
Potatoe chips
Cheese/peanut butter
  crackers
Baby food
In chewing gum
  (as a Mastic)

Remember that not all brands contain pork or a pork by-product, but I found some in each of the products listed. When shopping check the labels when you are purchasing any of the above and make sure the one you choose to buy does not contain pork.

About whole wheat bread; just because the bread is made from whole wheat flour and looks brown, do not assume it is made with something other than hog. You must develop the habit of checking each and every label on everything you buy.

Detergents, cleansers and *dish liquids* also contain pork. (Enzymes) You will be able to tell which ones do not contain pork by the Kosher symbol which will be on the box, the can or the plastic bottle labels.

Never use anything that lists the contents as containing *animal fats* or *animal shortening.* To date scientists have classified almost a half-million species in the animal kingdom and there is no accurate way to determine which one of these half-million animals are in your foods, cosmetics or medications. It's best to pass up these products and search for one that at least identifies the animal used to make it.

If a food, cosmetic or medication says "fatty acids" put on your brakes. There are vegetable "fatty acids" and there are animal "fatty acids." Fatty acids are used mostly as anti-caking agents in numerous blends of ingredients. Fatty acids usually means a fat pig. You would have to write the company to find out which one is being used in your product, but be very careful in your wording because experience has taught me that sometimes a manufacturer will tell you what they think you want to hear. So it's best to skip the "fatty acids" for now.

The next page gives samples of labels from foods containing pork/hog/swine to let you see how it is listed on the ingredient label.

Look for *lard, animal shortening, shortening, gelatin, calcium, emulsifiers, stabilizers* and *protein.*

Now that you know what not to buy, let me give you instructions on what is safe to buy. Samples are on the next page. Purchase only:

> Pure vegetable shortening
> Partially hydrogenated vegetable oil
> 100% Vegetable oil
> > Soy bean oil
> > Corn oil
> > Palm oil
> > Safflower oil
> > Coconut oil
> > Sesame seed oil
> > Olive oil
> > Peanut oil

*Of course the ones lowest in Cholesterol are the best!

CONTAINS: ANIMAL FATS AND VEGETABLE OILS

Ingredient Listing: IF PLAIN: ENRICHED FLOUR (FLOUR, BARLEY MALT, NIA-CINAMIDE, FERROUS SULFATE, THIAMINE HYDROCHLORIDE, RIBOFLAVIN), SUGAR, PARTIALLY HYDROGENATED ANIMAL AND/OR VEGETABLE SHORTEN-ING (MAY CONTAIN ONE OR MORE OF THE FOLLOWING: BEEF FAT, LARD, SOY-BEAN, COTTONSEED, PALM AND COCONUT OIL), WATER, EGG YOLKS, WHEY, NONFAT MILK, SOY FLOUR, SODIUM ACID PYROPHOSPHATE, DEXTROSE.

Shortening

INGREDIENTS: Enriched wheat flour (contains niacin, reduced iron, thiamine mononitrate [vitamin B_1], riboflavin [vitamin B_2]), animal and vegetable shortening (lard and partially hydrogenated soybean oil with hydrogenated cottonseed, soybean or palm oil or coconut oil), salt, sodium bicarbonate, malted barley flour, calcium carbonate and yeast.

. A DELICIOUS BLEND OF SUGAR, ROASTED PEANUTS, CORN SYRUP, HYDROGENATED VEGETABLE OIL (CONTAINS ONE OR MORE OF THE FOLLOWING: PALM KERNEL, COCONUT, SOYBEAN, PALM, COTTONSEED, OR SAFFLOWER OIL), COCOA, SKIM MILK, SOY FLOUR, WHEY, SALT, SORBITOL, LECITHIN AND MONO AND DI-GLYCERIDES (EMULSIFIERS), NATURAL AND ARTIFICIAL FLAVORS, SODIUM CASEINATE (A PROTEIN), CARRAGEENAN (STABILIZER), CARAMEL COLOR.

CHOCOLATE FLAVOR FROSTED CEREAL+ MARSHMALLOW BITS

Ingredients: Flour, Animal Fat and/or Vegetable Oil Shortening (Contains one or more of the Following: Lard, Hydrogenated Palm Oil, Hydrogenated Soybean Oil, Beef Fat with BHA, BHT, Propyl Gallate and Citric Acid added to Preserve Freshness), Water, Corn Syrup, Salt, Whey Solids, Baking Soda, Sodium Bisulfite, Artificial Color (with FD&C Yellow No. 5).

READ

STUFFED IN HOG CASINGS

Ingredients: Beef, Water, Salt, Corn Syrup Solids, Dextrose, Flavorings, Sodium Erythorbate, Sodium Nitrite.

INGREDIENTS: SUGAR, GELATIN, ADIPIC ACID (FOR TARTNESS), DISODIUM PHOSPHATE (CONTROLS ACIDITY), FUMARIC ACID (FOR TARTNESS), ARTIFICIAL COLOR, ARTIFICIAL FLAVOR.   170 g

There, you have nearly a dozen acceptable oils with contents that do not contain the pig. I am including this list of acceptable fats and suggesting that you read and re-read the labels of these products until you recognize and understand exactly what's in the product you are seeking to eat and use. Look for *kosher* products. Kosher means right & proper. Look for the international symbols that denote a product as being pork-free. Samples of these symbols are on the next page. Study them. These symbols will be located either on the front in the right hand corner of the product or on the back. When you find this symbol on a product you do not necessarily need to read the ingredient contents because this symbol means pork-free. However, just to be on the safe side, read it anyway. Things change.

The Kosher symbol is also a good way to tell what kind of calcium is used in a product. Some calcium, emulsifiers, poly-sorbates, monostearates, magnesium stearates and glycerides are made from a vegetable origin, but unless the product is marked kosher/pareve, you are probably getting these additives from the hog.

I had a very scary moment when I discovered a ruling saying that a vegetable oil may contain animal fat and still be labeled vegetable oil as long as it contains more vegetable oil than animal fat. I believe this is one of the reasons some oils list as *Vegetable Oil* and others read as *Pure Vegetable Oil.* Look for the kosher symbols whenever possible. Product wording can be tricky.

Cheese is another questionable food because cheese can contain Gelatin or Rennet. *Rennet* is a natural enzyme which curdles milk or forces the solids into precipitation to make a cheese product. Animal *Rennet* is most often used in commercial cheeses. *Rennet* comes from the digestive system of the hog and other young mammals. Swiss cheese does not contain animal *Rennet.* It's best to purchase your cheese from the health food store since most cheese labels do not reveal their Rennet content or tell you where it's from, or look for the kosher/pareve symbols on the outside of the pack. Of course Gelatin listed on a cheese label is a no-no.

Another way to shortcut the system and handle the supermarket blitz of hidden-hog is to just ask directions to the kosher section. American Jewish citizens who have remained Kosher (hog-free) shop in this section, or if you're

KOSHER
[pork-free]
LABELS

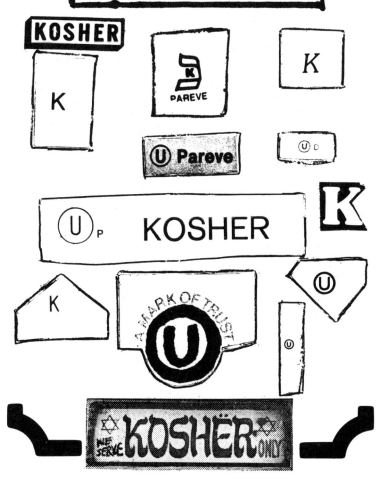

what you're LOOKING *for—*

"*Kashruth* [the Jewish dietary laws set forth in the Bible] in its highest form,"

INGREDIENTS: ENRICHED FLOUR (FLOUR, NIACIN, REDUCED IRON, THIAMINE MONONITRATE [VITAMIN B₁], RIBOFLAVIN [VITAMIN B₂]), VEGETABLE SHORTENING (CONTAINS ONE OR MORE OF THE FOLLOWING PARTIALLY HYDROGENATED OILS: SOYBEAN, COTTONSEED, PALM, PEANUT), MALT, SALT, BAKING SODA, DAIRY WHEY, YEAST.

made with PURE VEGETABLE SHORTENING

No Sugar Added No Preservatives

BAKED WITH 100% VEGETABLE SHORTENING

INGREDIENTS: SYRUP, MOLASSES, SALT, PARTIALLY HYDROGENATED VEGETABLE OIL (ONE OR MORE OF: COTTONSEED, COCONUT, SOYBEAN AND PALM), ANNATTO COLOR,

NO SALT

Made with BEEF

INGREDIENTS: WHEAT FLOUR AND STARCH, HYDROLYZED VEGETABLE PROTEIN, BEEF FAT, SALT, ONION, CARAMEL COLOR, NONFAT MILK SOLIDS, MONOSODIUM GLUTAMATE, SPICES, GARLIC, DISODIUM INOSINATE AND GUANYLATE.

NATURAL INGREDIENTS

contains no sugar, no artificial flavor, no colorings, no stabilizers, no emulsifiers, no additives, no preservatives, no added salt.

No animal derivatives.

really gung-ho go and visit a Synagogue library and gain a generous supply of information regarding a pork-free existence. However, this book contains everything you'll ever need to know about how not to eat pork and live a life without the pig. Amen.

SWEET-TOOTHING

When it comes to sweeteners, honey is a better choice over processed sugars, because the commercial granulated sugars offered on the grocery shelf are made by being filtered through *animal bone charcoal* before it is crystalized. Right. You guessed it; they use hog bones for this purpose. Both beet and cane sugars are made this way. Some raw sugars are not processed like this but you will have to check by writing the sugar company and finding out which brands are kosher/pareve. There are a few. Sugar is also hidden under a variety of aliases.

> Sucrose
> Dextrose
> Maltose
> Glucose
> Lactose
> Fructose
> Molasses

Our most recent addition is Aspartame, a chemical that resembles the taste of sugar. It's too new, too widely used and not tested enough for a person who is trying to eat right to use. I wouldn't touch Aspartame with a ten foot pig. Not yet.

I have one final comment to make about sugar. If sugar is powerful enough to rot teeth enamel which is made of the hardest substance in the human body, then you can just imagine what it does to other body tissues which are much softer.

COSMETICS/TOILETRIES AND MEDICATIONS
Containing Pork By-Products:

Now this was an interesting area to investigate. This area of consumer use is indeed fantastic. I have not knowingly

43

eaten any pork for almost 20 years and even I found some things that I had not been aware of as a result of not using certain products.

It seems that the cost of a cosmetic or toiletry has very little to do with whether or not it contains a pork by-product. It's in some of what is considered the very best brands in department stores to the cheapie kind on the corner drug counter. Since pork is used primarily as a preservative in its by-product category it appeared as the animal of choice for beauty products designed to keep us young looking. It also is used heavily in the hair pomade and hair perming industries. It apparently preserves the curl and set better than anything else cosmetician chemists have discovered.

The following page will give you a perfect idea of how widespread the use of the pig is in cosmetics, medications and toiletries. You'll have to read the ingredient labels on these products too. Designer and generic brands.

There are some who argue for the pig and say that when in the chemical stage that pork is not harmful, but what is the point of giving the pig up as food if you continue to use it all over your body and in your homes? No point.

These ingredients come from the pig's pancreas, from the liver, brains, glands and fat of various bovine animals. Some is even taken from the horns, hooves, feathers, quills and hair of animals. Gelatin (lard) is most prevalent which comes from the internal fat in the abdomen of the pig. Is is used because it is easily absorbed into the skin of humans. It is also made from boiling the skin, tendons, ligaments or bones in water (pig parts).

When searching for pork in medications both Over-The-Counter, (OTC), and those requiring a prescription, I was most disappointed with our pharmacists. I went to umpteen drug stores and hospitals across the country and was very discouraged to find that most pharmacists do not know all the ingredients in the medications they dispense. Neither do the doctors. For the most part when I asked them to give me the names of the drugs/medications derived from the pig they looked at me in a kind of wonderment. The majority seemed to not even understand the question. Apparently they had never been asked that question before. The only drug they readily knew of that was derived from the pig was Insulin, which comes from the pig's pancreas glands. No amount of prodding elicited any further answers about the pig. They knew the chemical contents of drugs but not the animal. Tsk. Tsk. Tsk.

Not knowing of anyone else who was qualified to define the drugs and medications containing swine by-products, I was forced to read the entire two-thousand-three-hundred and seventy-five leafed *Physician's Desk Reference* myself, page by page. The PDR is a book produced each year by Medical Economics Company giving the names, ingredients, indications, reactions and brands of every prescription and non-prescription drug or medication on the market. There are over 5,000 to date. It was very informative reading and I found tenebrous baleful proof of the pig hiding in several medications.

COSMETICS & TOILETRIES
CONTAINING PORK OR PORK BY-PRODUCTS*

Shampoos	Skin Lotions
Hair spray/Hair spray oils	Face cream/Facial Masks
Wrinkle Removers	Body Rubs/Jels
Hair Conditioners/rinses	Hair Permanents
Setting Lotions	Toothpaste
Liquid Make-up/Rouge	Hair Dyes and Hair Colorings
Bath and Face Soap	Cold Wave Preparations
Hair Dressings/Pomades	Lipstick
Nail Polish	Shaving Cream/Pre-shave lotions
Acne Preparations/ Creams	Mascara

While checking the ingredients in cosmetics and toiletries I found a few other interesting sounding contents:

Horse Tail Extract	Placenta Extract (whose?)
Japan Wax	Nettle Extract
Colt's Tail Extract	Calcium Lake
Aluminum	Mink oil

*All of the above contained:

Hydrolyzed animal protein, Gelatin, Collagen, Tallow, Stearic acid, Cholesterol, Hydrogenated animal glycerides, Hydrolyzed protein and Amylase, Arachinonic Acid, Carotene, Isopropyl myristate or Keratin or Oleic Acid.

I hope the physicians and pharmacists who couldn't answer my questions will read this book to find out what they are prescribing and dispensing. They may eventually treat a patient like myself who wants to know what's in everything that has to be swallowed. The following will describe the medications and their functions.

MEDICATIONS, Prescription and Over-The-Counter DRUGS MADE FROM PORK

Insulin	Made from the pig's pancreas gland (beef avail.)
Pill capsules	Made from gelatin
Shiny coated pills	Covered with a thin gelatin coating
Calcium	Crushed hog or other bovine bones
Chymotrypsin	Used to promote healing and remove dead skin tissue
Thyroxine and Thyrotropine	Thyroid preparations made from the pig's thyroid
Mucin	Made from the pig's stomach for treatment of ulcers
Pepsin	Used for indigestion in stomach coaters (enzymes)
Epinephrine	Used to treat heart disease from pig adrenal glands
Progesterone	Extract from pig ovaries used for menopausal syndromes
Acth (Adrenocorticotropin)	From the pig's pituitary glands used to treat Leukemia and cystic fibrosis, gout and arthritis.
Adrenalin	From the pig's adrenal glands
Heparin	From the pig's intestinal mucosa, for blood clotting
Gelatin tablets	Made from the pig alledgedly to promote nail growth
Pancreatin	From the pig's pancreas used as a digestive aid and for chronic pancreatitis.
Corticotropin	A gel used with injections (gelatin) (Veg. avail.)
Levothyroxine	Used for thyroid dysfunctions (from the pig's thyroid)

Others were:	Anti-fungal treatments
	Nutritional supplements for oral
	or tube feedings
	Dermatitis ointments, soaps
	and preparations (acne)
	Rabies Vacines
	Vaginal suppositories and creams
	Indigestion mixtures and chewable
	tablets/Antacids
	Baby formulas

VITAMINS (in bottles, plastic containers and snap-out tabs)

Unfortunately there is also a lot of hog floating around in our vitamins, liquid supplements and tonics. The pig spares no category of human consumption. If the label says:

	Protein	(from what?)
(bone meal)	Calcium	(from where?)
	Dessicated liver	(whose?)

Watch out! Dessicated means dehydrated (dried up) in order to preserve. The capsule size pills (and the round ones) are coated with a thin, shiny, resinous covering. This covering is referred to as "Pharmaceutical Glaze" which is a shield of gelatin used to keep the contents of the pills intact. "Pharmaceutical Glaze" is too vague a description. You may think you are swallowing a pure element of vegetarian, herbal or mineral origin and it turns out to be just another form of pork. As I have explained; people in high and low vocational positions do not always understand what is actually a form of pork, nor relate routine medication staples to being made from the pig. This is why we must learn how not to eat pork so we do not rely entirely on others who may have only limited or misinformation on a plethora of products.

The exact contents of all prescription and OTC drugs should be documented and made public with the drugs containing animal by-products listed separately with alternative choices. I wonder why this hasn't been done yet. You cannot get well taking medications which contain poison.

The use of pork by-products in our medicines gives further rise to the already hallucinatory impression that pigs are immortal and necessary to our survival. But they are not. Active dissatisfaction will produce a change in these conditions in our pharmaceutical products. A few of the more amusing contents in various drugstore medications were:

Irish moss
Pregnant mares' urine
Ox bile extract
Sherry wine
Root beer
Oyster shells
The Perrywinkle plant
Arsenic
Ducks' embryo
Root of Rauwolfia Serpentina

Some medications used the term "made from small bovines" and even though they didn't specify which "bovines" I would be leary of those too.

Try it for yourself, ask your pharmacist to tell you some of the medications made from the pig, or any other animal. Listen to what they tell you.

I visited two scientific laboratories which perform medical and other research studies on the pig. I found them to be used in testing infant formulas based on scientific claims that the baby pig's nutritional needs are similar to the human baby's. All of the studies using the pig's flesh had to be performed in temperatures under 40°F Because the souring bacteria (pork worms) quickly multiply if not near frozen during testing procedures. They were also used in studies on alcoholism since pigs very easily develop a taste for ethanol and will abuse it if given the chance. How about that, a drunken pig. Out in the country areas they hold pig relay races, pig swim meets, roasts pig barbeques, make hoghead stew, liver mush and boiled lungs.

My most surprising discovery was finding some farm children in the mid-west who use the pig's bladder for a toy ball. They take it out, dry it, blow it up and bat it around. They said they're extremely durable. I believe them because pigs have a rough tough hide — both inside and out. They also use pigs as pets (kiss them), give them awards at country fairs, and feature pigs as prizes at carnivals.

Another company has a "Pig Mail Order Catalog" filled with clothing, jewelry, and household decorations all using the pig, his shape, and head as a customized emblem. Other generalized uses for the pig are as follows:

ACCESSORIES MADE FROM THE PIG OR PIG BY-PRODUCTS

Shoes	Livestock feed
Wallets	Shoe polish
Adhesives	Pet foods
	(pig lungs and spleen)
Linings of Shoes	Candles
Purses	Fertilizers (the waste
	from the waste)
Carpet padding	Textiles
Hats/caps	Paper
Jackets	Photographic paper
	and film
Gloves	Cork
Insulation	Industrial lubricants
Upholstery Stuffing	Dunnage or packaging

The pig seems to make something out of nothing. The sow's influence on the American society and economy is more expansive than I even imagined.

After reading over these lists you will recognize that it's entirely possible that 85% of the entire American population begins and ends each day utilizing the pig. Consider this as an example:

You awaken in the morning and take a shower with soap that contains tallow, wash and condition your hair with a concoction containing hydrolyzed animal protein, brush your teeth with toothpaste made of pig calcium, lotion your face with a cream made with protein, put on pig skin shoes, eat bacon or sausage for breakfast, have a ham and cheese on rye for lunch, pork chops for dinner and a few lard ladened cookies as a bedtime snack — you will have used the pig all day long. Who would have ever thought that these daily routine motions could all be linked by one common bond — the hog?

This is a very simple appraisal to make. Pick a day, any day, and check out everything you eat or use on your person.

See how many of them contain pork or a pork byproduct. This is called the *Sunrise to Sunset Pig Test.* You may begin.

Note:

If you discover any other products made from the pig write and tell me about them so I can include them in future reprints of this book.

Do not continue to defend the pig. They are not a relative or personal friend. We don't owe the pig anything. They are only an animal and a filthy one at that.

SCRAPPLE?

Formerly an old-fashioned food for old-fashioned Philadelphians, scrapple is on the verge of making a comeback that is taking new Philadelphians by their pork scraps — so to speak.

The Historical Society of Pennsylvania presents an evening of tastes and talk on this unique combination of meat, meal and spices. "Scrapple or Philadelphia Pate?" will be presented tomorow at 5:30 P.M. at the Historical Society, 1300 Locust St.

Gourmet dishes using scrapple will be prepared, along with information relating to the history of scrapple in this country — one that began 300 years ago.

List of Subjects in 9 CFR Part 94

African swine fever, Animal diseases, Exotic Newcastle disease, Foot-and-mouth disease, Fowl pest, Garbage, Hog cholera, Imports, Livestock and livestock products, Meat and meat products, Milk, Poultry and poultry products, Rinderpest, Swine vesicular disease.

Accordingly, 9 CFR Part 94 is amended as follows:

Background

The regulations in 9 CFR Part 94 (referred to below as the regulations), restrict the importation into the United States of certain animals, meat, and animal byproducts in order to prevent the introduction into the United States of various diseases, including rinderpest and foot-and-mouth disease. Section 94.4(b) sets forth the conditions under which a person may import cooked meat (except meat sterilized by heat in hermetically sealed containers) from ruminants or swine originating in any country where rinderpest or foot-and-mouth disease exists.

Executive Order 12291 and Regulatory Flexibility Act

We are issuing this rule in conformance with Executive Order 12291, and we have determined that it is not a "major rule." Based on information compiled by the Department, we have determined that this rule will have an effect on the economy of less than $100 million; will not cause a major increase in costs or prices for consumers, individual industries, Federal, State or local government agencies, or geographical regions; and will not cause a significant adverse effect on competition, employment, investment, productivity, innovation, or the ability of United States-based enterprises to compete with foreign-based enterprises in domestic or export markets.

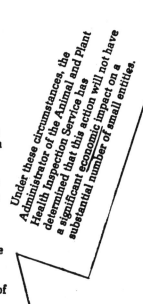

PART 94—RINDERPEST, FOOT-AND-MOUTH DISEASE, FOWL PEST (FOWL PLAGUE), NEWCASTLE DISEASE (AVIAN PNUEMOENCEPHALITIS), AFRICAN SWINE FEVER, AND HOG CHOLERA: PROHIBITED AND RESTRICTED IMPORTATIONS

Under these circumstances, the Administrator of the Animal and Plant Health Inspection Service has determined that this action will not have a significant economic impact on a substantial number of small entities.

CHAPTER VI

HOW TO SEASON YOUR FOOD WITHOUT USING PORK

The kitchen should be the cleanest room of the house since this is the area where food is prepared and often eaten. A kitchen utilized for the constant preparation of hog — STINKS! They carry an unpleasant odor. This pungent aroma attacks the curtains, cabinets, walls and appliances. When you enter a house where pork is cooked daily you can immediately smell it. No matter how much disinfectant or room ventilation is used, you cannot expunge or blot out the odor of the hog.

In homes where it is only cooked occasionally it's much easier to clear the air of the scent of freshly cooked hog. If you cook and eat anything long enough, pretty soon you become so accustomed to its' odor that you cease to be aware of it.

I have visited in the homes of pork-eaters and they fry pork bacon and save the grease (oil) off the bacon to cook their "greens and beans" in later. They would pour this hog juice over their other foods for seasoning. This practice is a big part of the addiction to the taste of hog. It is used interchangeably in all kinds of dishes as seasoning.

I once heard a schoolteacher's reply when one of her students queried her about not eating pork. Her response was: "It's silly to try to stop eating pork because there's just no way around it." This particular teacher held a Masters degree in elementary education. Witnessing this instructor-pupil dialogue made me realize that maybe even our children are being taught to accept the pig, based on the fact that the public at large does not have any idea about how to stop eating it (some teachers included). Of course this was only one incident. The other teachers I talked to refused to be pinned down on the subject long enough to give me a straight answer on why the detrimental aspects of eating pork was not taught or discussed in science or health classes. One science teacher did let me in on the news that subjects like pigs are usually reserved for college where small bovines are dissected and studied. College is much too late to teach young people about the horrors of eating pork. By then our young have been thoroughly indoctrinated to the taste of the swine and are hooked by the time they reach college age. This teaching has to literally start in the crib.

If you are not going to eat pork or use it to season your foods, then what are you going to use? There are many inexpensive ways to season your foods without pork. You can use:

> margerine
> liquid corn oil
> real butter
> beef or chicken bouillion cubes
> safflower oil
> A slab of beef fat trimmings

All of these will give you that "greasy" taste that many enjoy in their foods. The above supplements will satisfy this desire and needless to say they do not contain the scabby hide of the pig. Some other ways to season your vegetables is to use a couple of slices of beef bacon, beef neck bones, or beef steak bones. Another way to season your food is to use *spices:*

Cloves	Curry
Garlic	Bay leaves
Oregano	Sage
Parsley	Poultry seasoning
Paprika	Dill
Tumeric	Tarragan
Pepper	Chili powder

You don't have to be a gourmet cook to start using spice in your food. They are sold at practically every supermarket and do not require refrigeration. Your vegetables may taste a little odd at first but eventually you'll get used to the wholesome new taste, and will enjoy them even more when you remember how much cleaner your food is as compared with the way you used to eat. Try upgrading your taste buds with foods seasoned only with spices or a low-cholesterol vegetable oil. Try them all until you develop the combination that suits you best. Don't use ham hocks (pig knuckles) or other pieces of the pig's mangy hide. Eat the leanest of the beef and leave the biggest part of the fat on your plate. But if you must use "fat meat" then use some that comes from a cow or a chicken.

If right now you were to stop reading this book and get up and go into your own kitchen and throw out all the items which contain pork or a pork by-product — you would probably be out of food and have to return to the store to purchase more. There would be few items left in the refrigerator or the cabinets. Do this investigation anyway and then check around at your friend's and relative's houses. This test is called the Pick-Out-The-Pork test and in order to pass it you have to be able to distinguish between the items which contain pork and the items which do not. Pork is in about 50% of all the foods in the grocery store — no matter what state you reside in.

Wives can help to preserve their husbands or mates to live a much longer time by ceasing to cook pork filled meals. Women are still in charge of more kitchens than men and most spouse/mates will pretty much eat whatever is set before them, so the head cook can be directly in charge of helping to make this change in diet. But whether the chef decides to cook pork or not is a moot point when it comes to self survival. You still have to take control of your own stomach and your own mouth, both at home and abroad regardless to whomever is cooking.

Do not use pork meat grease to cover up and drown out the natural nutrients present in fresh vegetables. The fat you have been using is the liquified pig flesh filled with microscopic parasitic worms. This liquified flesh is more sticky than greasy. (like pus)

Would you pass a dead animal on the highway that has decomposed to the point of having live maggots crawling around in it, stop your car, go over to the dead animal and shove your mouth and face down in it? Of course not. But that's exactly what you do every time you bite into a piece of pork.

Breakfast is no problem. It is quite simple to replace pork with better choices. For the more industrious I have included a short recipe on how to make your own beef sausage at home:

> 1-2 pounds ground beef (clean)
> 1 tsp. salt/optional, salt substitute
>   may be used
> 1 tsp. black pepper or cayenne
> 1 tsp. honey
> 2-3 tsp. of sage (to personal taste)
> Mix these ingredients together and season
> to your own particular taste.

This sausage can be cooked immediately, frozen or made into patties and used for burgers also. Beef sausage is available prepackaged, so is beef bacon. Already prepared and ready to be cooked.

If you decide to invest in a sausage stuffer be very careful in the choosing of your casings to be used to stuff the sausage in. Some are synthetic and can be eaten, others are synthetic but can't. Read your label instructions and examine how the casing peels off the meat to determine if it's edible. A lot of the wieners, sausage and luncheon meats are stuffed into hog casings. If so, it should say so on the wrapper. Also be very careful about purchasing ground beef because if you do not personally see it ground you can't be sure of exactly what was ground. Try to at least purchase your ground beef in a grocery store that does not grind their own sausage but buy it from dealers who have already prepackaged it for retail sale.

It's interesting to note that a lot of people who continue to eat pork do not smoke cigarettes or use tobacco. But what sense does it make to stop smoking to keep the tar and nicotine out of your lungs, and not stop eating pork to keep the worms out of your muscles? None. I talked to a few excercise instructors in YMCA and YWCA gymnasiums who said they did not believe that pork had any influence on good health, "as long as you cook it done," and impugned the reality of parasites actually living inside their bodies. Others said "I've been eating it so long, I can't stop now." Why can't you? It's not like giving up water which is required to maintain life. A persistent hog-eater may decide it's not necessary to give up pork, but neither is it necessary to bathe, but we bathe to keep filth *off* our bodies, and we stop eating pork to keep filth *out* our bodies. Both actions are part of what is necessary to claim being in-good-shape and living a clean life.

Anyone who professes to be intelligent cannot continue to eat the pig's unhealthy flesh after learning what it really is. No learned or educated person would knowingly eat something called "hog-head-cheese" made of crushed ears, nose and mouth mucous, gristle, ground up tongue, rotten gums and pus from any animal, and definitely not a pig. We would not eat these parts from any other animal and the beef and poultry industry knows this, which is why they don't offer cow-head-cheese or chicken-head-cheese. Plus, those animals do not contain the gelatin (pus) to make their meat congeal like the pig's does.

To this point I have not addressed "soul food" and find no need to elaborate on this silly slogan. The information in this book dispels the need for any people to hang on and claim ownership of eating "low" on the hog as a reminder of the validity of their cultural heritage. There are more righteous qualities in all of us that are more important to promote and retain than the eating of pig guts.

Stores seem to practice a type of "pork class distinction" when stocking pig parts in their meat departments. I found pig tails, feet, ears, stomachs, intestines, heads and knuckles in smaller grocery stores and in poorer sections of a community. Apparently poor people are still more apt to eat "lower" on the hog than wealthier ones.

In the more sophisticated areas the stores stocked pork roasts, hams, chops, brains (considered a delicacy), pork tenderloins and the like which are considerably more expensive than those mentioned above. I saw very few affluent looking shoppers purchasing pig heads or feet. Classy people who eat pork still eat "high" on the hog.

Some stores carried both the high and low parts of the pig but they rarely displayed them in the same spot in the freezer.

All of the processed and luncheon meats are stocked in the same area usually along with the bacon, bacon rind, scrap bacon and rolled sausage. You have to look carefully to distinguish them.

There is only one area where pig parts are mixed and that's in magazines. Many of our more bourgeois publications which feature recipes for holidays or daily meal planning will include pork in their itinerary of preparation ingredients. In fact almost every magazine on the rack relating to diet or cooking includes the pig in some form or fashion. Make up your own recipes if necessary and the very next time you go shopping remember to choose one of the flavorings I have suggested to season your foods.

SUMMARY: This notice announces the Food Safety and Inspection Service's (FSIS') intent to permit producers of dry cured or country ham not currently using one of the two prescribed methods for destroying trichina in pork to continue to use nonconforming methods beyond the effective date of August 6, 1985. This approach will both protect consumers and permit dry cured or country ham producers to continue production while research concerning the effectiveness of current processing techniques is undertaken.

A final rule prescribing a third method for destroying live trichina in dry salt cured hams and which could also be used for country hams was published on February 7, 1985 (50 FR 5226), and is effective August 6, 1985. With the development and publication of the third method, FSIS believed it had addressed *all* dry curing methods currently in use. However, FSIS has recently learned that many of the smaller dry cured or country ham producers use methods which still do not meet the requirements of either of the two prescribed methods. These producers use ambient temperatures that may not meet the time/temperature requirements; use a curing process that does not include a mid-cure re-exposure of the ham to salt (overhaul); wash the ham before the required curing time is completed; or in some way do not meet the requirements. For several years, the Agency has permitted the use of nonconforming processing methods since they were traditional, decade-old methods believed to be effective in destroying trichina.

Because of the inability of certain producers to meet the effective date and since there have been no reported cases of trichinosis from products not treated under the three prescribed methods, FSIS, is permitting processors of dry cured or country hams utilizing trichina treatment methods not incompliance with 9 CFR 318.10(c)(3)(iv) to continue production.

-OR-

60

CHAPTER VII

HOW TO AVOID EATING PORK IN PUBLIC RESTAURANTS

Eating out. This section is a real tickler for non-hog eaters. There are those who maintain they have learned the science of "eating out" and therefore are able to do so successfully. Another groups asserts there is simply no way to do it — so they don't. Your personal conscience will have to be your guide on this one. If you decide not to eat out of anyone else's kitchen then more power to you, and you won't be interested in this chapter. ON the other hand, if you really enjoy the outing, the atomosphere and service of eating out, then read on.

The first requirement is to choose a "high class" looking establishment. You are less likely to eat any pork accidentally in one of these places than at Jack's Rib Parlor down the block.

Look at the tables, the chairs, the waiter's costume while waiting to be served. If there is that tell tale sign of grease residue on the furnishings, then you can be sure the place is off limits and taboo for a non-hog-eater. But if it looks clean, smells clean and appears well attended to, then proceed on to check the menu.

In reading the menu check to see how many types of pork the restaurant serves. Next check the number of fried foods because it's possible they interchange the hog grease and vegetable oil for frying. Find out if they broil or grill their steaks, then find out what other kinds of meats are cooked on the grill.

When you begin to ask these kinds of questions your waiter will become perturbed and look at you as if you just escaped from the funny farm. But never you mind, just plow right ahead with your questioning and request to speak with the head chef if need be. You might even want to take a quick peek at the kitchen. You have every right to ask as many questions as you please regarding the preparation of food-stuff you are about to consume and pay for. Be civilized in this and you will be successful.

Grilled cheeses, grilled meat sandwiches, etc., are not good choices because pork bacon or sausage is fried on this same grill during the breakfast period. Always insist on having your food broiled and not fried.

Be sure that you do not receive a premixed salad, the waitress may have just used the knife or sandwich board to cut up a bacon-lettuce and tomatoe sandwich, or slice a ham sandwich in half. The new make-your-own-salad bars are a God-send for a non-hog-eater dining out. You get to see what you get and get only what you see. Again, check the utensils at the salad bar. Make sure you don't use a dipper that's been in the gelatin dessert, cottage cheese or synthetic bacon bits made of soy protein and possibly flavored with pork.

Back at the table continue with your examination by checking your coffee cup and water glass for a grease line. This grease may have come off of the silverware or may have already been in the cup or glass which tells you in any event that either the dishwashing equipment is not too effective or that they serve a lot of greasy food (probably hog) which does not easily wash off.

It may seem rude to others but when in doubt, smell your food when it's served. It's your stomach, body and life that's at stake so make sure you know what you're getting. Pork has it's own peculiar, rank, almost ammonia type smell which can be detected with a quick sniff if necessary.

In finer restaurants all vegetables are cooked in plain water with as little salt as possible. Sometimes it's better to call a restaurant beforehand and ask all the right questions before you decide to go there for a meal. It'll save a lot of time at the table and you'll feel more confident.

It's best not to order desserts or ice cream because it's too risky. Food distribution places have to prepare food fast and preserve it for as long as they can, and you know by now that hog is the most abundant preserver for foods and cosmetics today. Gelatin makes stale food look perky for a longer period of time. Those beautiful designer pastries on the dessert tray may have been made the week before yesterday. Remember to open your mind and mouth and ask questions. Better restaurants welcome your inquiries.

ON THE JOB

At work a well known associate may go out of their way in trying to be helpful and surprise you by bringing you a hot lunch or sandwich. You may be exceptionally busy working on some special project and your colleague, being thoughtful, drops a package on your desk directly in front of you — anticipating your gleeful surprise at their remembrance. You peek in the bag, or styrofoam tray, and instantly recognize food containing pork or from a carry-out that specializes in "swine to go."

This is a tough one. What do you do?

In order not to appear ungrateful or make a statement that will make you lose the amicable companionship of a considerate co-worker, and blow your concentration for the rest of the day; do one, two, or all of the following:

1. Peep in, make some kind of exclamation about how good it looks (it may)
2. Sincerely thank the bearer and offer to pay them for their trouble.
3. Suddenly lose your appetite (depending on what's in the package you might anyway)
4. Explain how busy you are and that you don't want to lose your momentum by stopping to eat and will put it away until later.
5. Push the package aside and quickly change the subject — talk fast.
6. Wing it.

One of these solutions should work, keep you from embarrassing the giver, ostracizing yourself, and thereby save the job relationship.

Occasionally you will be offered some "homemade" goodie prepared by the office "baker" perhaps even made especially for you on some special day. Resort back to the above techniques. A hearty thank-you is in order.

To further complicate these food related vocational traumas there are always certain individuals who derive some sort of weird pleasure or satisfaction from seeing others eat. They'll usually stand around the desk insisting that you taste it immediately. Right now! Don't. Talk about your diet, tell them you're off sugar (which you should be). Accept it if you

63

a-b-s-o-l-u-t-e-l-y must, then throw it away on your way home. (Not in the office wastebasket, someone might find it and make the announcement). As a very last resort, if push comes to shove, say no-thank-you and explain why. This same rule applies to refreshments at office parties.

Be comforted with the knowledge that unique dietary habits are very popular and still on the rise, so you certainly have a lot of truthful options to avoid sticking a gift pig in your mouth.

For those "knowledgeable" co-workers who tell you that the trichinae worm is not present in all pork — explain there is no sound basis for that assumption which is why the public is warned and advised to cook *ALL* pork well done. This is to make sure that the only trichinae worm you eat is a cooked one. In addition to the fact that heat does not guarantee the killing of all pork worms, remember that the larva are very tiny and you can unknowingly swallow several hundred of them. When the natural warmth and even temperature of your body envelopes them, they dissolve and become free to go about the task of growing and breeding further in your body. To suffer the symptoms of pork worm poisoning you need not eat but one pregnant parasite.

CHILDREN AND YOUNG ADULT ACTIVITIES

Nursery and Pre-School

Do not rely on the nursery attendants to properly feed your child. I found many of their menus fictional. At today's baby-sitting rates you have every right to request that your toddler be fed only the food that you bring each day. Take foods cooked in boilable plastic bags, reheatable containers or thermos jugs. Take your own cookies, juice or other snacks. Give your instructions to the owner, the supervisor and other charge attendants. Repeat your instructions on the initial application form and on the medical sheet.

Kindergarten

Teach your children about the pig and pork at the earliest age possible. Show it to them in the supermarket. By the time they go to elementary school they will be trained to stay away from pork. Teach them to refuse everything away from home except milk or fruit. This can be done painlessly. Let them take a bag lunch if they desire a mid-day meal with the rest of the children. Explain your requirements to the teacher and the principal. Be pleasant. Hold them responsible. The word will get around.

ELEMENTARY SCHOOL

Your children do not have to miss out on class celebrations, festivities or birthday parties just because they don't eat pork. For school parties you can donate clean cookies or purchase pastries from a kosher bakery. Again, explain your specifications to each homeroom teacher each year that your child attends public or private school.

At this level it's also a good idea to have a short informative chat with the cafeteria cook and school dietitian. Public schools serve pork routinely in a variety of ways so actually it's best to let your child brownbag it. Obtain a cute lunch pail, let your child pick it out. Check the school menues and you *may* decide to allow your child to eat on "certain" days — only after you have toured the school kitchen. As a taxpayer you have access to all public school territory. At private schools the tuition is so high you have access because of what it's costing you. Be nice and everyone concerned will cooperate with your wishes.

BIRTHDAY PARTIES

One good way to control this situation is to feed your child before they go to a party and instruct them as to which chips, pretzels, fruit or beverages they may partake of. You may want to serve cake and ice-cream for dessert after dinner so your child will not miss out on these tasty treats and can enjoy them pork-free at home. Explain your wishes to the parents of the birthday child and instruct them not to ostracize or point out your child about not eating certain things. Check out the party menu and leave kind but explicit instructions — or stay at the party and help serve and supervise. The parents will be grateful for the help. After the 3rd grade your child should be thoroughly trained on how not to eat pork and will be proud of maintaining a clean diet and being special.

Your child's present health, behavior, and future well-being is at stake; so it's well worth this extra effort to protect your offspring from receiving any pork. They will still enjoy the games and prizes.

HIGH SCHOOLERS
Let them read this book.

CARRY-OUTS:

These days when more and more consumers are declining to eat the scavenger pig a lot of bar-be-que houses have added beef ribs to their menus. But if you are really serious, which I hope by now you are, then do not eat the beef ribs if they have been cooked on the same grill as the pork ribs. Hog has a very powerful distinctive odor and taste. Hog will drown out anything else it's added to so it's not a good idea to eat beef ribs prepared on the same grill as the pork ones. To do so defeats your purpose.

Fast food restaurants took a nose dive during 1984. All but a few of them inducted the hog into their menus. Breakfast spots rose up all over America serving ham and biscuits, sausage and biscuits, bacon and eggs, etc. Then came the bacon burgers, bacon covered baked potatoes and ham and cheese omelettes. I was saddened to see this preeminence of pork.

Trying to eat breakfast in a restaurant is another deal altogether. To begin with, breakfast is not a good time to go out to eat publicly if you are striving to be a non-hog-eater. This period in restaurants is always clouded with pork bacon, sausage and fried ham. The eggs are fried in this grease, the grits are stirred with the same utensil used to make the pancakes and turn them over. Your best bets are:

> Waffles (cooked on an appliance)
> Oatmeal
> Fresh fruits/melons
> cold cereals
> Toasted English muffins/swiss cheese

If you're at a party and your hosts are serving food look at some of the guests. There are always one or more persons who sit down at meal time and immediately start to literally bite the table. Devouring everything in sight, smacking their lips in glee. After they finish, in between licking the plate, they mumble "that was delicious, what was it?" Take time to find out what you're eating. Don't just gobble up everything in reach just to be polite or show your hosts you're grateful to be getting a free meal.

Always take your food to a lighted area before you start chomping. Never go for pot-luck dinner invitations or community smorgasbords because most of the dishes will contain some type of pork. Above all, if at a party you should accidentally discover a juicy piece of bacon hidden under your cole slaw, don't jump up and attack your host, or slam your plate against the closest dining room wall. Excuse yourself, find the nearest restroom and proceed to gag yourself. You'll have to move fast to make it. Better yet, you can save yourself the hassle of having to upchuck away from home by just eating before you arrive. If you decide to tell your hosts you are on a pork-free diet this can be a good way to break the ice at a party by creating a lively discussion about diets, health, exercise and the like. Be aware though that I have attended parties where as soon as I started a discussion about pork many people just up and leave the room. They didn't want to hear about the pig. The truth always runs falsehood away. These pork proponents did not just leave because of disinterest, but because of their inability to prove the validity or justify the eating of pork. Of course I'm always grateful when hog-eaters ask questions or show an interest in seeking information to change their eating habits. The next time you go to a party mention pork and see what happens. Watch the most animated and party-people clam up in a knot. The discussion of pork always comes off as a kill-joy issue. Observe this for yourself, but don't be cruel and corner a hog-eater at a party just to watch one squirm. Our job is to teach, not to taunt. Over zealous fervor is just as bad as blithe ignorance. Let's not be heartless about this.

Teaching your children to handle school lunch trays, junk foods or visits to fast food chains will require skill. It's best to only allow them to eat out when you are with them until they reach such an age or point to be able to read the hidden meanings of symbols in public food preparation.

Eating out can be a very enjoyable experience if you heed all the warning signs right in front of you under your nose.

If after all of these precautions you still manage to swallow some of this poison (pork), it serves you right, because by now you certainly realize that the hog has rooted its way into every crack and crevice of American life. If you should eat some, the human body has a built in siren to alert you to this disorder. The moment the pork touches your lips you will feel a tingling, almost menthol like sensation on the mouth and tongue. This odd sensation will progress as it passes down your throat into your stomach. Your previously clean digestive system will rebel and react violently to the re-introduction of poison (pork). Once this poison reaches your stomach is rests for a while notifying the entire body of its presence before moving on. A few minutes later you will experience very hard gripping pains in the lower part of your stomach (similar to those felt after taking a harsh laxative) the pains will increase. Your stomach will attempt to throw off (regurgitate) this unwelcome visitor but it will be too late by them. You'll have to suffer through the entire trip with the hog as it passes through your body. The average distance from your mouth to your rectum is about 26 feet in length but if you're in pain during the passage is seems more like 26 miles. Your body will retch with its futile attempts to send it back upstairs (through the mouth) but will eventually accept the post of having to propel it out of the other end of the body (through the bowel sack). As this pork travels through the intestines the severe discomfort is caused by this poison shoving everything out of its way. Your whole body will break out in a profuse sweat as it gets in a hurry to eliminate this waste. The moment you get the urge to release your bowels you won't have a choice. Things will seem normal at first and then you'll experience a sort of blasting effect as this poison pours out of you dragging everything else you had in your stomach and digestive tract along with it. From then on the symptoms will be those of diarrhea, extreme nausea and emesis. Your blood pressure will have shot sky high and your head will ache. No other food creates this type of physical reaction.

I guarantee anyone that after this mind (and body) blowing experience you will proclaim to the world that pork is really and truly poison.

Of course a hog-eater who has been nibbling on pork since the beginning of time will have built up an immunity to this reaction, but if you have been off all pork for 30 days or more — this is exactly what will happen to you. I can tell you from both observation and experience. This is the very worse feeling in the world. Likened to pneumonia, intestinal virus and the flu all rolled into one. It's a bad trip. This is not a fabricated description.

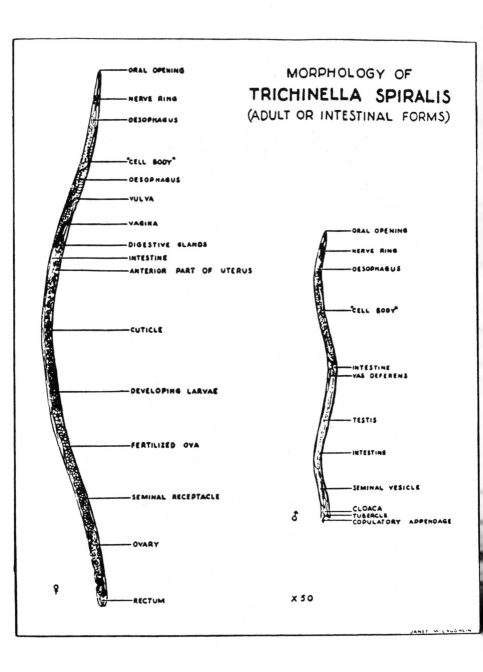

MORPHOLOGY OF
TRICHINELLA SPIRALIS
(ADULT OR INTESTINAL FORMS)

ORAL OPENING
NERVE RING
OESOPHAGUS
"CELL BODY"
OESOPHAGUS
VULVA
VAGINA
DIGESTIVE GLANDS
INTESTINE
ANTERIOR PART OF UTERUS
CUTICLE
DEVELOPING LARVAE
FERTILIZED OVA
SEMINAL RECEPTACLE
OVARY
♀
RECTUM

ORAL OPENING
NERVE RING
OESOPHAGUS
"CELL BODY"
INTESTINE
VAS DEFERENS
TESTIS
INTESTINE
SEMINAL VESICLE
CLOACA
TUBERCLE
COPULATORY APPENDAGE
♂

X 50

JANET M. LAUGHLIN

69

CHAPTER VIII

HOW TO SURVIVE WHEN VISITING FRIENDS AND RELATIVES WHO EAT PORK

No matter how hard you try to prevent it, there will arise those unavoidable occasions when you will wind up at a friend or relative's house during mealtime. This is a very sensitive situation. A non-hog-eater should not be rude or uncivilized, but at the same time one cannot compromise on the principles of correct diet by eating pork in order not to offend someone.

No matter how much you love your family and friends and do not want to hurt their feelings, the rejection of pork has to have first consideration and top billing.

You can start by trying not to ever be present. When this fails, (as it inevitably will), if you have the funds try inviting everyone out to dinner, or offer to go after a bucket of chicken. If you go to the store yourself then you will be in charge of what you buy and what's in it.

If you're going to have to spend any extended length of time staying with hog-eaters rush out and go shopping yourself and purchase items that do not require extensive cooking or the use of several pots and pans. The quicker you can get in and out of the kitchen, the better. Be pleasantly firm.

Of course, if they are close associates you may just tell them that you are not eating pork anymore. However, if your hosts are purebred hog-eaters they will not like the idea that you do not eat what they eat. They will protest and try to make you feel small, or try to shame you into joining them in their hog. Don't fall for tears, threats or the cold shoulder. Remember that it's your body and your life. Stick to your guns and they will either comply with your wishes and respect you, or never invite you back again. Either result makes for a hog-free success for you.

I have visited places where I had to take my own pots and pans, because if you eat out of their dishes and pots which have been washed in their hog-greasy water, then you are again defeating your purpose. If they have a good dishwasher, with very hot water, then you *might* decide it's safe enough to use their cooking and eating utensils. Otherwise, paper plates work fine.

I once visited my cousin and her husband for a weekend stay a few years ago, they are both hog-eaters and I anticipated problems in handling the eating arrangements. I certainly appreciated their hospitality and wanted very much to spend some time with her — but she was caught between a rock and a hard pig, because she didn't know how to inform her husband that I would rather they didn't cook or eat any pork during my stay, versus telling me that she could not change her family's eating habits just for me . . . her cousin. Far be it from her to realize that I only visited them once a year, but they both refused to give up their pork eating for even one weekend — out of the remaining 51 available to them after I left. So strong was their allegiance and addiction to eating pork. Not wanting to create any discord between she and her husband — I promptly left the next morning and spent the remainder of the weekend in a clean atmosphere at a friend's house who did not eat pork. As much as I love my cousin, and her husband, I could not in good conscience tolerate their pork eating and cooking in my presence. This was a very difficult choice for me to make. It always will be when you have to chose between a loved one and a pig-free surrounding. But always choose the pig-free surrounding. They'll get over it.

If your alternate choices are limited and you find yourself stuck somewhere overnight, there is a 100% chance that you will awaken to both the beautiful morning sunlight and the putrid aroma of cooking hog being prepared for breakfast. Closing your door at night helps some and prevents a great part of this odor from infiltrating your clothing and bed linens. Carry your own room spray, this also helps to dispel pork odors — at least temporarily. Take your own soap, toothpaste and lotion.

The best remedy for the away-from-home-morning-hog-blues is to get up before everyone else and make the breakfast yourself. Don't cook any of your own food in their ovens because they most surely have been used to bake a ham or pork roast. The swine grease will have hardened on the inside of the oven and melt when the oven gets hot, and the strong penetrating powers of the hog will attack and cling to anything else you are cooking in that same oven. Never, ever use their skillets. They will be tainted with years and years of frying pork bacon and pork sausage. Don't use their toaster either, it may have bread particles in it that have come from making toasted bread containing lard or animal shortening.

Definitely — do not go on a picnic with hog-eaters while visiting. They always, always, always, will bar-be-que pork spareribs, pork weiners or the like. If the picnic is on a holiday or at a public park, you can count on about 50 to 100 other families all cooking the same thing — hog. There will be no clear air for you to breathe and you'll develope a headache from the smell. Beg off. Don't attend.

Don't get angry with your family or friends but refuse to let them trick or shame you into eating pork after you've stopped.

During my on-the-street interviews I would stop and question several people in major cities. (like New York, Philadelphia, Newark, Chicago, Atlanta, Baltimore, Miami, Los Angeles and Cincinnati to name a few) Incidentally, Cincinnati, Ohio is nick-named Porkopolis because it reigns as the Pork center of America. Anyway, I would question people until I found someone who claimed not to eat pork, but said they ate it "occasionally." I asked on what occasions and to explain to me what they did when they were served pork at a friend's house or at an important business dinner? Do you know what they overwhelmingly replied? They said "I eat it." I asked why, and the general consensus was: "I (we) don't want to offend anyone, or be rude." One guy (a Ph.D.) told me that he had instructed his wife and children not to make a big issue out of not eating pork when in the public or while in someone's home as a guest. Several said they were quite uncomfortable about declining and ended up eating "just a taste" anyway. The rest of the respondents seemed nervous and appeared not at all at ease in even discussing how they handle rejecting pork away from home.

This is a terrible terrible situation, allowing yourself and your family to be manipulated by hog-eaters who have a natural disdain and disregard for anyone who tries to give up eating pork.

Any so-called "friend" who tries to force you into eating pork when they know you have given it up is not a "friend" anyway. No matter what a person tries to do to better themselves, a "friend" will support their efforts, learn what they can, and perhaps do the same instead of expressing outrage or resentment. When you tell your friends you are not eating pork anymore you are going to be surprised at how fragile some egos are as many of them will take on an attitude of "you're trying to be better than me." (which turns out to be the truth). Those "friends" who are determined to eat pork and insist on eating it in your presence are not worth using any unwholesome words on. Just give them one of those silent looks that in body language means you-are-so-silly! Works every time. You may decide to elicit the company of other non-hog eaters, then you can talk openly and share your experiences.

With pork, it's every man, woman and child for him or herself — so don't worry about the die hards. This is exactly what they'll do — die, hard, if they continue to eat pork.

After you learn enough tact to deal with meal time problems, then comes the next and equally important task of how to handle kisses and hugs from hog-eaters.

Being civilized is still the key behavior in this matter.

As an example, if someone pushes a baby or toddler towards you for an embrace and kiss, who has visible swine grease on his or her cute little face; obviously you don't want to shove the kid back or blurt out: "I don't kiss babies with hog on their face." This might sound a bit hostile or rude and would certainly insult the parents. A way to avoid this is to duck and press your nose into the child's stomach or chest being sure to aim your head away from their face. Hold the baby out in front of you and twist it around a little and this will be construed as being an affectionate gesture and keep you from having to make facial or lip contact with the pork on their little kissers.

Adults present a different kind of a problem. Obviously it won't look very normal to bend over and press your face into the stomach or chest of another adult, and if they are a real hog-eater you definitely won't be able to pick them up. So don't try it. It's best to turn your face aside as far as possible, and give them a hearty hand shake and a mild squeeze hug, all the while murmuring UMMMMMM-UM. This will usually satisfy a normal person's quest for receiving an affectionate welcome while at the same time protect your face from coming into contact with hog covered lips.

Protect your face and mouth at all costs. If everything else fails, grab their hand, shake it briskly and say: How you doin'?, you sure are lookin' good! This definitely will inflate any ego long enough for you to be able to move on to other appropriate conversation and offset the kiss or hug.

Be creative, experiment, try different approaches until you learn to move quickly and think fast in these situations. This will require a lot of tact and attention so as not to be caught off-guard unprepared and get lip smacked with a hog flavored kiss.

A WORD OF WARNING

If you are deadly serious about not eating pork and staying away from it in all forms, this next important piece of information may possibly change your entire love life.

If your mate, fate, or date is a hog-eater and you have not been able to convince them to join you in your hog-free crusade, then your problems are just beginning.

If you are having any type of intimate contact in the form of kissing, sexual intercourse, or other, with a person who is eating pork regularly; then you may as well abandon your own efforts towards a pork-free existence, if you continue to deal with them.

Be aware that the trichinae worm multiplies after entering the system so the severity of contamination is directly related to how much and how often the host eats pork.

The normal mucus in the body is derived from what one eats, and any orifice in the body that secretes any substance has a distinct odor and consistency indicative of that person's diet. If you are not eating or using pork, then you do not want it on your tongue, inside or outside of your sexual organs or on your hands, etc. etc. That's right. If you want to remain hog-free then don't sleep with a pork eater and you will avoid receiving any pork second-hand through sex.

If you are currently having relations with a pork eater, then most assuredly you are sharing in that person's hog. There is now way around this, especially when you consider that the hog-eater can have several extra pounds of this excess mucus in their bodies from consuming pork daily. Spend a little extra time thinking about this. It makes sense.

This test is called the *Supreme Pig Test.* If you pass this one you've got it made, because your resistance against the pig cannot be swayed or penetrated by love, beauty or physical contact.

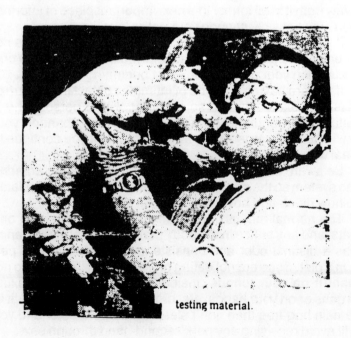

testing material.

possible AIDS-pork linkage

THIS ARTICLE IS COPIED FROM A COLUMN WRITTEN BY MR. JACK ANDERSON OF WASHINGTON, DC IN NOVEMBER OF 1985 REGARDING A POSSIBLE AIDS-PORK LINKAGE.

WASHINGTON:

SOME MEDICAL RESEARCHERS SUSPECT THE FEDERAL GOVERNMENT IS DISCOURAGING TESTS THAT MIGHT IDENTIFY A DEADLY SWINE VIRUS AS A CAUSE OF AIDS, FOR FEAR THAT SUCH A REVELATION WOULD WRECK THE PORK INDUSTRY.

U.S. RESEARCHERS HAVE DISCOUNTED RESEARCHERS SUGGESTIONS OF A CONNECTION BETWEEN AIDS AND AFRICAN SWINE FEVER VIRUS, SAYING THAT ALL GOVERNMENT TESTS HAVE PROVED NEGATIVE. IN FACT, THEY SAY, NO CASES OF AFRICAN SWINE FEVER HAVE EVER BEEN FOUND IN U.S. PIGS.

BUT WHILE OFFICIALS CLAIM THE SCIENTISTS ARE SOUNDING NEEDLESS ALARMS, MANY RESEARCHERS CHARGE THAT THEIR WORK IS BEING IMPEDED BY THE AGRICULTURE DEPARTMENT, WHICH CONTROLS THE MATERIAL NECESSARY FOR THE SWINE FEVER TESTS.

THE DEPARTMENT "IS AFRAID THE PORK INDUSTRY WOULD FAIL IF AFRICAN SWINE FEVER IS RELATED TO AIDS," DR. BELDEKAS OF BOSTON UNIVERSITY TOLD REPORTERS.........

BELDEKAS SAID HE HAD BEEN ORDERED NOT TO TALK TO THE PRESS FOR NATIONAL SECURITY REASONS, BUT HE CHARGED THAT AGRICULTURE OFFICIALS HAVE BEEN LEAKING WORD OF HIS RESEARCH TO .....FARMERS. "I HAVE BEEN DIRECTLY THREATENED BY PIG FARMERS," HE SAID.

SOMETHING FROM THE AUTHOR...

"How Not To Eat Pork" was released in
June of 1985. Since that time I have
traveled extensively around the country
promoting this book on television, radio
and in bookstores. It is an exciting
campaign wherein I have encountered
every reaction from disbelief and shock
to open hostility. Eating pork is a
perpetual hot topic. Everywhere.

Reviews of "How Not To Eat Pork" have
been routinely excellent and
devastating. Some are critical of my
writing style and credentials for lacing
such a serious subject as trichinosis
with dashes of entertaining humor. No
reviewer has ever claimed that my book
is boring, although in some circles I
have been charged with spreading lies
about a tasty meat and innocent animal
Bunk.

The greatest greatest proof
of the validity of my findings occured
after my book hit the stands; FDA
approved the pork industry to use
irradiation to try to kill the trichina
worms in pork. We know that it is
economically unfeasible for a company to
spend millions of dollars on radiation
equipment to eliminate a nonexistent
problem. We ask, if cooking pork kills
the trichina worm, and if pigs are no
longer fed garbage, why is radiation
necessary? Radiation is pretty powerful
stuff, especially when its being used to
solve a problem that FDA claims to have
conquered over 50 years ago.

Several major news programs demonstrated apprehension and outright refused to cover my personal appearances or book parties. Initially certain magazines contacted me to do a story on my research but later quietly backed out of the interviews. Each refused to discuss why they cancelled. Due to the popularity and economic impact of this book on the pork industry they have increased their advertisements and stepped up their promotions especially in ethnic publications. Talk shows such as Phil Donahue and Oprah Winfrey, and the rest, refuse to take my charges seriously, even after the pork industry decided to try to x-ray the worm out of the meat. Viewer demand and letters will gain recognition of the pork problem and provide national coverage about the dangers of eating it.

Additionally, the connection between the horrifying disease of AIDS and Swine Fever was announced globally and then quickly hushed up. Other medical findings proving various ailments to be caused by eating pork surface almost weekly.but continue to be ignored by the press, doctors and the public.

This book is the first and only one of its kind that uncovers the real truth about pork, and reveals the lies consumers have been told strictly for economic gain. We must run this killer-meat from among us if we want to have a healthy, happy and long life.

And thank you for reading this book.

Media

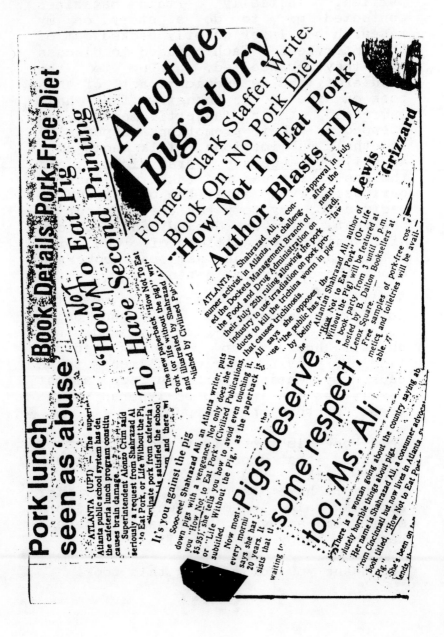

Another pig story

Former Clark Staffer Writes Book On 'No Pork Diet'

"How Not To Eat Pork"

Author Blasts FDA

Lewis Grizzard

ATLANTA - Shahrazad Ali, a consumer activist in Atlanta, has challenged the Dockets Management Branch of the Food and Drug Administration on their July 25th ruling allowing the pork industry to use irradiation on pork products to kill the trichina worm in pig ducts that causes trichinosis. Ali says she opposes the use of the public has approval in July after the near-radiation law

...being Atlantan Shahrazad Ali, author of "How Not to Eat Pork" (Or Life Without the Pig) will be featured at a book party from 3 until 5 p.m. hosted by B. Dalton Booksellers at Lenox Square.

Free samples of pork-free cosmetics and toiletries will be available.

Book Details Pork-Free Diet

Not To Eat Pig

"How Not to Eat Pork"

To Have Second Printing

The new paperback "How Not to Eat Pork (or life without the pig)" written by Shahrazad Ali and illustrated by Civilized Publishing is...

Pork lunch seen as 'abuse'

ATLANTA (UPI) — The superintendent of the Atlanta public school system has determined the cafeteria lunch program constitutes brain damage...

Superintendent Alonzo Crim said he seriously a request from Shahrazad Ali to "How Not to Eat Pork, or Life Without the Pig, eliminate pork from cafeteria... satisfied the school... there was...

It's you against the pig

Sooo-eee! Shahrazad Ali puts down pigs with a vengeance. Not only does she tell you "How Not to Eat Pork" (Civilized Publications, $5.95), she tells you how to avoid even touching it, as the subtitled. "Life Without the Pig," as the paperback...

Now most every morning she has says 20 years. It sists that th waiting to...

Pigs deserve some respect, too, Ms. Ali

There is a woman going about the country saying absolutely horrible things about pigs. Her name is Shahrazad Ali, a consumer advocate from Cincinnati but now lives in Atlanta She's authored a book titled, "How Not to Eat Pig." She's been on...

Woman not hog wild about pigs

There is a woman going country saying absolutely things about pigs.

Her name is Shahrazad sumer advocate who is fro but now lives in Atlanta. ten ook titled. "How Por The on talk microscope author filled frie laboratory slides should pork. Plus, free samples cosmetics and toiletries will be The book is also available at the AUC bookstore.

Well, h are li

pork produc sandwiches and pork rinds (meat sn and I don't think worms in my brain person.

AROUND THE REGION —

Guard fighter jet crashed into a safely, setting the structure ablaze and leaving at dead, one injured, and one missing. Ali, the author of How Not to Eat Pork, has accused Public School System of child abuse for serving meat causes brain damage, but school officials said there will menu changes.

nose nad be years ago perfectly There and her

ntelligent: they've ev as well as rs the a

1985

There is a woman going ntry saying absolutely ut pigs. ne is Shahrazad ow lives in ocate who book

Author hogs limelight

The Atlanta Journal AND CONSTITUTION

Shahrazad Ali saying things about pigs

LEWIS

Pigbusters Have Arrived !

ATLANTA — A new book: How Not To Eat Pork (or life without the pig) written and illustrated by Atlantan Shah- razad Ali (Shah-Rah-Zod Ah- promises to end the con

firm; Civilized Public Pork," endorsed · by int acclaimed health s Gregory of the Safe Bahamin D This book up-to-date medi-

BOOK NOTES

come to their defense. Basically what Ms. Ali

Shahrazad Ali, author of "How Not to Eat Pork," will participate in a debate with a repre- sentative from the Food and Drug Administra- tion on Friday at 1:30 p.m. at Benjamin E. Mays High School in the auditorium. Ms. Ali will also vited. Ms. Ali will autograph copies of her book at B. Dalton Booksellers in Southlake Mall on Saturday from noon to 1:30 p.m.

ATLANTA — A new book: To Eat Pork — written and Shahrazad and Ali illustrated by Atlantan How Not pork (or life without the pig) How Not To Eat Pork for all 24 p published by a new Atlanta firm International Publications dealer Dick Gregory of the famous book not only reveals up-to medical facts against eating pork you how to avoid it in any and

if by a ra and son y swam out in the mention the the pig

 once a afternoon, saved my li was the b

if you eat pork products ly to get worms in your

unce of pork you eat as, "has the trichina

en to this: I have products, such andwiches 1 pork

No pork, please, is theme of new book by Atlantan

81

SOMETHING ABOUT THE AUTHOR

Shahrazad Ali (Pronounced Shah-Rah-Zod Ah-lee) is a freelance writer and consumer advocate specializing in political, social and health subjects. She has worked in various capacities in the medical specialities of Neurology, Urology, Opthalmology and Pathology for over 18 years. Her experience as a concerned parent regarding a pork-free diet, coupled with years of research, study, laboratory tests, and physician and patient contact, qualify her to be an authority on the usage and affect of the pig in America. How Not to Eat Pork (or life without the pig) is the resultant thesis from these investigations. She is the proud mother of three children and resides in Atlanta, Georgia. Mrs. Ali has eliminated pork from her diet for over 20 years.

ABBREVIATED
BIBLIOGRAPHY

The Complete Diary Food Cookbook — 1982
E. Annie Proulx and Lew Nichols

The Special Guest Cookbook — 1982
Arlene, Heidi and Sandee Eisenberg

The Hog Book — 1977
Jerome D. Belanger

Diseases of the Swine — 1975
Dunne & Leman

Live Longer Now — 1974
Pritkin, Leonard & Hofer

How To Eat To Live — 1972, Books 1 and 2
Elijah Muhammad, Messenger of Allah

Physician's Desk Reference — 1984
Medical Economics Co. (PDR)

The Hog — 1977
Thomas P. James

Book of the Pig
Jack D. Scott

The Meat Book — 1973
Travers Moncure Evans & David Green

Back To Eden — 1939
Jetho Kloss

The Hog, Should It Be Used For Food? — 1936
C. Leonard Vories

The Book of Living Foods — 1977
Edmond B. Szekely

Bailey's Industrial Oils and Fat Products — 1979
  Edited by Daniel Swern
  Fels Research Institute, Temple University

Principles of Meat Science — 1975
  Edited by B.S. Schweiger
  Forrest, Abdele, Hedrick, Judge and Merkel

Protein Resources and Technology — 1978
  Status and Research Need
  Edited by Milner, Scrimshaw and Wang
  Sponsored by the National Science Foundation

Kashruth, Handbook for Home and School
  Union of Orthodox Jewish Congregations of America
  Rabbinical Council of America

The Complete book of Bacon — 1981
  William J. Hogan

Quality of Pig Meat, Progress of Food and Nutrition
  Science — 1981
  Jul, Mogens and Zeuthen

Pig Production in the Tropics — 1979
  Devenda, Canagasaby and Fuller

Pork Industry, Problems and Progress — 1968
  David G. Topel

Trichinosis in Man and Animals — 1976
  Charles C. Thomas

Trichinosis — Report on an Epidemic — 1947
  F.H. Hathaway and L. Blaney

Trichinosis, Clinical and Laboratory Observations in a group
  of 256 Cases — 1947
  Oppenhein, Whims and Frish

Trichinosis and From His Tail to His Snout
  A. L. Manous

Little Pigs Birthday — 1984
  Marcia Leonard

Pig Management & Production — 1982
  Derek H. Goodwin

Biology of the Pig — 1978
  Wilson G. Pond and Katherine A. Haupt

Diseases of the Swine — 1975
  Edited by H.W. Dunne and A.D. Leman

The Pig as a Laboratory Animal — 1971
  L.E. Mount and D.L. Ingram

Pigs from Cave to Cornbelt — 1950
  Charles Towne and Edward Wentworth

A History of Domesticated Animals — 1963
  F.E. Zeuner

Pigs — Wild and Tame — 1979
  Alice L. Hopf

Wonders of Pigs — 1981
  Sigmund A. Lavine and Vincent Scuro

Foodborne and Waterborne Diseases — 1981
  Their Epidemiologic Characteristics
  I. Jackson Tartakow, M.D., M.P.H. and John H. Vorperian,
  B.S.

The Food Additives Book — 1982
  Nicholas Freydberg, Ph.D. and Willis A. Gortner, Ph.D.

Oils, Fats and Waxes — 1895
  Books I, II and III
  Dr. J. Lewkowitsch, M.A., F.I.C.

Modern Soaps, Candles an Glycerin — 1906
  Leebert Lloyd Lamborn
  3rd Edition

The Food Additives Dictionary — 1981
  Dr. Melvin A. Benarde

The High Blood Pressure Book — 1979
  Robert J. Glaser, M.D.

The Complete Family Guide — 1981
  To living with High Blood Pressure
  Michael K. Rees, M.D.

Sugar Blues — 1975
  William Dufty

How to Cook A Pig — 1977
  Betty Talmadge, Jean Rabitscher and Carolyn Carter

Medicine for the Layman — Heart Attacks — 1981
  U.S. Department of Health and Human Sciences — Dr.
  Robert I. Levy
  Public Health Services, Natl. Institute of Health

Evolution of the PlioPleistocene — 1979
  African Suidae
  Transactions Ser: Vol 69, Pt. 2

Pig Appeal — 1982
  Laurie Winfrey

SUMMARY

Well, I think that should just about do it. After reading this book you should be well on your way to a pork-free existence and be qualified to develop your own individualized game plan to keep from absorbing any pork whatsoever. I've given you the truth as your main ammunition. It is worth the extra effort to remove this filth from your life.

There are many many new diets on the market but none of them have given you the information contained in this book. My diet is not for weight-control, it is for life-control.

Everything in this book is true. It was a wise man who once said "the truth shall set you free." In this case it will free you of the blasted worm infested pig. Congratulations. You now belong to the elite class of Americans who are hog-free!

INDEX

==

MAIL ORDER FORM FOR ADDITIONAL COPIES FOR LOVED ONES

SEND TO:

CIVILIZED PUBLICATIONS
2019 SOUTH 7TH ST.
PHILADELPHIA, PA 19148

$10.00 Per Copy (Includes Postage & Handling) Cks. or M.O.

Number of copies_____   Amount Enclosed_____

NAME_____

ADDRESS_____

CITY/STATE_____ZIP_____

Wholesale rates available for individuals, stores, groups or
organizations ordering 10 or more copies.   Write for info.

THANK YOU